The Coercive Power of the Law

Riley Clare Valentine · Zane McNeill

The Coercive Power of the Law

Vulnerable Bodies and Boundaries of Perception

palgrave
macmillan

Riley Clare Valentine
Baltimore, MD, USA

Zane McNeill
Denver, CO, USA

ISBN 978-3-032-07588-8 ISBN 978-3-032-07589-5 (eBook)
https://doi.org/10.1007/978-3-032-07589-5

This Palgrave Macmillan imprint is published by the registered company Springer Nature Switzerland AG
The registered company address is: Gewerbestrasse 11, 6330 Cham, Switzerland

Acknowledgments

Riley Clare Valentine: I would like to thank first and foremost my family and friends for consistently orienting me towards other people. I would not have been able to complete this project without my community; I would not be who I am without the trans and disabled community. Thank you for everything. No person has ever gotten to where they are without others, and I want to especially thank Judy LaVergne, Nicklas Parker Benedix, Elizabeth Riley, Katya Wright, and everyone who has supported me along the way. Of course, without Zane this book would have been impossible.

Zane McNeill: I'm deeply proud of what we've accomplished with this book. Riley and I came to the project from very different disciplines and lived experiences, and I believe that this interdisciplinary patchwork of theory and ethnography is what makes the work unique. So much of legal training serves as an indoctrination into a system where, at worst, lawyers protect capital at the detriment of everything else, and at best, they act as tools of reform within a system that depends on that limited reform for its own sustainability. Riley continually reminds me that we can—and must—be more than that and I'm so grateful to Riley for helping me hold onto the ability to imagine worlds beyond our current capitalist hellscape—especially in a moment when it can feel impossible to believe in a future at all. While the text is often deeply critical and, at times, heavy, Riley's work on care infuses it with hope. It is, at its core, a labor of love—love for community, for people, and for the belief that law and governance can be more than just disciplinary or regulatory tools. So, thank you to them, to our ancestors that fought back against the law as a tool of repression, to my amazing dog, Crunchwrap Supreme, and to you, the reader, for believing that books can be a tool to dream new liberatory worlds.

Contents

CHAPTER 1

Introduction

Abstract The introduction to this book offers a critical exploration of the interplay between law, care ethics, and the body, emphasizing how legal systems both reflect societal values and regulate and discipline bodies and sexualities that deviate from normative standards, branding them as deviant or pathological. This chapter critiques the liberal notion of personhood as an autonomous, rational actor, highlighting its failure to acknowledge the fundamental interdependence and vulnerability of human beings. This liberal framework is shown to be inadequate for addressing issues such as reproductive rights and anti-transgender legislation, which reduce complex relational and embodied experiences to adversarial rights-based conflicts, obscuring the interconnected nature of human lives. Grounded in critical disability studies, queer theory, and Foucault's theories of power, the book challenges liberalism's focus on rights and autonomy, advocating instead for a framework centered on care ethics.

Keywords The body · Care ethics · Liberal personhood · The law · Critique of liberalism

The language of "being seen" is woven into the US cultural and legal landscape, individuals who want to be recognized by the law and thereby

R. C. Valentine and Z. McNeill, *The Coercive Power of the Law*, https://doi.org/10.1007/978-3-032-07589-5_1

by the State frequently underscore arguments for progressive legal reform. Yet, many bodies have often been seen and regulated by the law. As Michel de Certeau has written, "There is no law that is not inscribed on bodies. Every law has a hold on the body…Every power, including the power of the law, is written first of all on the backs of its subjects."[1]

Legal discourse has long functioned as a mechanism for defining and disciplining bodies, constructing categories of normativity and deviance. As Alan Hyde argues in *Bodies of Law* (2001), the law does not merely recognize pre-existing bodies but actively constitutes them, treating bodily autonomy, identity, and ownership as legal constructs rather than inherent, self-evident truths. Hyde interrogates how the law often perceives the body as property, illustrating how legal frameworks commodify, control, and lay claim to corporeality. "Constructions of the body enact or perform specific regimes of political relations," Hyde argues. "Different political domination is involved when the body is property owned than when the body is a legible narrative."[2]

If the law is an expression of a State's values, that raises significant questions and concerns. If we have qualms with the law, do we in fact have larger concerns? And if we want to change the law, are we in fact requesting a change of State values? Wendy Brown defines the State as, "a significantly unbounded terrain of powers and techniques, an ensemble of discourses, rules, and practices, cohabiting in limited, tension-ridden, often contradictory relation with one another," that is "a vehicle of massive domination."[3] These are the concerns at the heart of our book. We utilize queer theory and care ethics as our foundation to think through how the law impacts the lives of marginalized populations. We believe that the law has a direct obligation to citizens. The law ought to support mutual caring relationships, respond to needs, attend to individuals, and facilitate care. By this, we mean the law has a direct obligation to the people and to their common good. As Hyde explains, "another choice that legal discourse must make…is when to configure the body in relationship to others: to be seen, empathize with, touched…through physical contact with the body of another…in which the body represents human solidarity."[4]

Our legal analyses build on feminist theory, critical legal studies, and critical race theory, which challenge and disrupt mainstream legal thought. As Pheng Cheah, David Fraser, and Judith Grbich describe, mainstream legal theory is grounded in the idea that, "[R]ational social consensus is formed in order to protect and maximize basic person or property rights or dispositions… As a result, rationalist legal theory defines legal obligation as the acceptance of state coercion as a legitimate or rationally justified by each individual subject that internalises the states rules."[5] Our text extends what these scholars point as a shift in legal scholarship and recognizes that the law is ever present in our bodies and relations.[6] Other categorizations, such as sex and race are also inscribed onto bodies before birth and affect the legal construction of the body throughout life.[7] Therefore, our work builds upon the work of feminist scholars who have reoriented legal thought to address "the reality of the oppressive effect of existing legal norms on the corporeal reality of women's lives."[8] It also draws from critical race theory (CRT) scholars, "critique of rights reflects the concerns of a white, largely male elite with traditional ideas of the false consciousness of the masses and does not [engage] with the deep and embodied understanding…of the history of slavery, colonization, and racism which informs the politics and legality of race in America."[9]

Alongside these fields of legal scholarship, we also integrate critical disability studies. The argument that the law is an expression of the State's perspective and values is significant within critical disability studies.[10] The law has often regulated people with disabilities' lives, whether it be from their ability to have children or obtain access to public spaces. The law is ever present. Other categorizations, such as sex and race are also inscribed onto bodies before birth and affect the legal construction of the body throughout life.[11]

The law is not unchangeable, it is mutable and frequently a reflection of shifts in priorities. In the words of Christine M. Hassenstab "The chameleon nature of law is connected to the numerous functions of Law; laws might be grounded in the sociological, the political, and even – or especially – concepts of normalized morality and ethics."[12] In 1972, the Supreme Court placed a pause on the death penalty in *Furman v. Georgia*, in which it found the death penalty to be "cruel and unusual" punishment. In between 1972 and 1976, states began to revise their statutes to ensure the death penalty was not overly applied. After these changes, the Court reinstated the death penalty in *Gregg v. Georgia* (1976). Law may act as a negotiation between groups. In which suddenly a group of people, such as individuals on death row, find themselves to be hypervisible, and later, made invisible again. As the landscape of both law and society changes rapidly, we do not expect for this to be a cumulative or final work on law and its impacts, rather we envision this as a part of an ongoing discourse with both law and society. Legal categories are never fixed in and of themselves; they shift in response to political priorities, demonstrating law's mutability.

As Michel Foucault has said, "visibility is a trap."[13] Visibility is a form of power. The oscillation between hyper-visibility and invisibility reveals how visibility itself operates as a mechanism of control and discipline.[14] When certain groups—such as people on death row, trans people, people with disabilities, and others—are made visible, they are positioned as objects of scrutiny, regulation, and debate, often within the framework of the State's biopolitical control, or "the domain of life over which power has taken control."[15] This visibility is far from benign; it is a calculated act that marks these bodies as deviant, exceptional, or in need of intervention. In fact, Mia Fischer argues that "dominant media and legal discourses of trans visibility often negatively impact the material, lived realities of transgender communities," as increased visibility frequently comes with heightened exposure to State surveillance.[16] Yet, as legal priorities shift and societal attention fades, these same groups can quickly become invisible again, pushed to the margins of discourse and policy.

While much focus has been placed on the fetishization of visibility and the liberation of queer people through visibility politics, Foucault argued that the act of examination or surveillance produces a subject who is not striving for visibility but is instead compelled to be visible.[17] "The simple fact of being aware of one's visibility status – and not the fact of being effectively under control – efficaciously influences behaviour," as Andrea Mubi Brighenti, professor of social theory, explains.[18] The State's capacity to control visibility serves as a potent tool for asserting authority and maintaining hierarchy. By determining who is seen, how they are seen, and under what circumstances, the State not only disciplines individuals but also shapes societal perceptions of normativity and deviance. The cyclical nature of visibility—its emergence and disappearance—underscores its role as a mechanism for regulating bodies and shaping narratives about justice, punishment, and morality.

If visibility is an exercise of power, then we ought to ask if there is a way for this power to be shared, to empower all parties, or is this power ultimately a form of subjection. Care ethics is one framework that allows a reimagination of power. People who have been subjected to power, such as Carrie Buck who fought against the State's right to sterilize people with disabilities, have frequently resisted the State's power to regulate bodies. Moreover, they have resisted the law expressing that they are *less than human*. Joan Tronto has expressed care ethics as a theory in which the vulnerable are the ones with power. The people are the ones invested with the ability to assess and make demands of the State, members of their communities, and ultimately themselves.

A life without care is difficult to imagine, in large part, because we are all dependent upon care. Infants die without care. At various points in life we will need others to help us. Care is unique because it is about our relationships with one another, not necessarily questions of rights. Care is an inherent component of our experience of life, and those relationships can bring significant meaning to our lives. They can also be stressful and difficult. It is not always easy to care for others or to be cared for, and yet, repeatedly, we find that caring relationships are an important aspect of our shared lives.

Care ethics eschews the conception of marginalized minorities as always acted upon, as passive recipients of care. Ultimately, we live in communities with one another. L'Arche communities have been pointed to in disability critiques as places of mutuality.[19] Care is not a uni-directional practice; it is one in which relationships are understood as essentially relational. Care ethics asks us to assess our own actions and selves, as well as the State, through our relationships toward one another. It rejects liberal arguments in which rights may be posed in opposition to one another, as in the case of abortion, rather we are asked to interrogate our relations as ones in which beings are understood as dependent, vulnerable, and inherently dignified.

Care ethics as a political theory extends the assessments to that of State action and inaction, its responsiveness to vulnerable populations, and whether it compassionately attends to its citizens. We do not exist as siloed off individuals. We are all vulnerable, and it is this vulnerability which connects us. It is also these vulnerabilities which have become the subject of regulation and separation.

Against Rights

Liberalism as a political and legal philosophy holds up a political actor who is independent, rational, and autonomous. It is embedded in the United States, with Thomas Jefferson's infamous statement in *The Declaration of Independence,* "We hold these truths to be self-evident, that all men are created equal, that they are endowed by their Creator with certain unalienable rights, that among these are life, liberty and the pursuit of happiness."[20] Jefferson lays out the tension inherent to liberalism—we are all equal and we are all free. If we prioritize equality within our politics, then we cannot be as free as liberals would like. Likewise, if we prioritize freedom, then some are free to be unequal. This problem rests at the heart of liberalism, and it is one that liberalism is woefully unable to provide us a guide to resolution.

The Founders' perspectives of rights is vastly different from the one most Americans hold. Jamal Greene, in a historical study of American rights, writes that the Founders believed rights ought to be sorted by communities themselves, and not judges.[21] Good governance should reflect the community's judgment, and if the community is just then it would protect the rights of all community members due to their participation and inclusion in the community. However, the Founders limited who was a part of the political community, particularly Black people, indigenous people, and women.

The Civil War and the resultant Reconstruction Amendments contributed to a shifting in the perception of the role of rights, and Justice Oliver Wendell Holmes, author of the *Buck v. Bell* decision which will be discussed at length in the second chapter, contributed to our modern conception of rights. Greene calls this perspective "rightist." Holmes grew up in an aristocratic family, spending time with authors and journalists such as Walter Lippmann, a noted contributor to neoliberalism. Holmes believed the law ought to lack moral commitment, "On the Holmes model, the judge decides whether a right is special, like racial equality or free speech. If it is, the judge looks skeptically at laws infringing the right. If it isn't, the government can do what it wants."[22] This keeps moral issues on the fringes of the law, and divorces cases from their larger social and ethical issues. Eugenics, which Holmes avidly supported, was not only a theory. It was an active sociopolitical program that sought to eliminate people with disabilities from society.

The "rightist" model, to use Greene's language, "outsources rights recognition and enforcement to judges, who are not well suited to performing the sensitive mediation needed to reconcile the rights of diverse citizens."[23] Judges who view and understand themselves as sifting through the Constitution to give guidance on contemporary debates over rights may not make decisions that are grounded in the concerns of their communities. Judges write decisions that may impact the entire nation, and this power cannot be overstated.

The American rights-based approach is posed as resolving conflicts. Jefferson's antinomies are interpreted as binary choices, rather than as possibilities that can be mediated. This peculiarity with American liberalism necessitates both political and ethical attention; the problem with liberalism is particularly salient in terms of abortion access. Abortion is frequently approached as a struggle of rights—the rights of the pregnant person as opposed to the rights of the fetus. The pregnant person and the fetus are immediately at odds with one another, perhaps even in a battle of legal recognition. If the pregnant person "wins," the fetus "loses." Justice Kennedy adopts this perspective in *Gonzalez v. Carhart*, where he argues, without evidence, that a person may experience "severe depression and loss of esteem" after their abortion.[24] Kennedy's argument occludes the relational aspect of pregnancy, that makes it an entirely unique decision. Abortion and pregnancy cannot be distilled into a battle or a game with winners or losers. Rather, it must be examined in terms of care.

We are more than rights-bearing creatures, ever seeking to assert ourselves, perhaps at the risk of others' rights. Often we see within rights-based discourse the possibilities for people who can never be the liberal political actor understood as less than. Disabled people have frequently been the site of this discourse. Trait Specific Abortions (TSA) are abortions which are undergone due to a fetus having a trait for a disability that is determined through genetic testing.[25] Many disabilities may be diagnosed before birth, such as sickle cell disease, cystic fibrosis, hemophilia, and Down's Syndrome, among other disabilities. Adrienne Asch, alongside other bioethicists, note that frequently TSAs are framed as a way to free a possible parent from a disabled child, "The medical professions justify prenatal diagnosis and selective abortion on the grounds of the *costs* of childhood disability – the costs to the child, to the family, and to the society."[26] To abort a future disabled person is to exercise one's rights and freedoms to be free from the burden of a disabled child. These professionals fail to note what others, such as Chris Kaposy and Hans Reinders, note—that parents of disabled children find parenthood to be a transformative and joyful experience, albeit different. Reinders writes, "They have to accept what nobody wants to accept; they need to live with uncertainty… They need to learn to celebrate achievement where many others fail to see that there is any."[27]

TSAs express a liberal perspective that a full life is one in which one is rational, independent, and an autonomous actor fully able to exercise their rights. It occludes a conception of a meaningful life that is vulnerable and one where we may be continually bound to another person. Indeed that life is posed as something that can never be fulfilling. And within liberal societies, the State has limited responsibilities to these families. Rights-based thinking places the responsibility for care upon the carers who may fully exercise their capacities of reason. This isolation is a grim mirror, highlighting a societies' lack of care for disabled people.

Ultimately, individuals ought to be free to make reproductive decisions without the burden of a lack of care and aid from the State. If the State absconds its responsibility to promote and protect caring relationships so that a person or a family is unable to care for a child that they would otherwise have had, the TSA becomes a coerced decision. Eva Feder Kittay, scholar activist, writes, "perhaps it is more appropriate to question how the larger society values or devalues disabled life – by looking at the resources it withholds or devotes to children with disabilities and their families – than to impute disregard for the value of the life of disabled persons to the pregnant woman who tests for and aborts a fetus with impairments."[28]

It is not our intention within this book to criticize individuals who are placed into coercive positions. We begin from a perspective that all beings are deserving of respect and care; all beings are imbued with dignity. It is thus unconscionable to place a person into a situation in which they may make a decision which they otherwise may not have made—whether that be aborting a possibly disabled child, to hide one's gender and sexual identity for fear of losing one's job, or stopping a child's hormone therapy due to the fear of being investigation for child abuse by child protective services. Within a rights-based discourse, we lose sight of the vulnerability, grief, pain, and loss at the heart of these experiences. We distance ourselves from the realities of a lack of care.

The emergent and sweeping trend of anti-LGBTQ+ legislation throughout the United States is a reminder that even if we *are* rights-bearing creatures, if those rights are revoked or are undermined, we have lost our capacity to be ourselves. Florida's infamous "Don't Say Gay" bill, HB 1557, heralded numerous copycat laws. After the passage of this law, Florida saw an exodus of LGBTQ+ families who had the ability to leave—56% of the respondents to a UCLA School of Law Williams Institute 2023 report left the State. 88% of LGBTQ+ families were worried about the effects of the bill, and a quarter of the respondents stated they have experienced harassment or increased incidents of harassment since the bill's passage.[29] HB1557 is infamously unclear, stating, "Classroom instruction by school personnel or third parties on sexual orientation or gender identity may not occur in kindergarten through grade 3 or in a manner that is not age-appropriate or developmentally appropriate for students in accordance with state standards."[30] This law has been interpreted in many different ways, whether it be the removal of children's books with parents of the same gender, or teachers changing their titles from the gender-neutral Mx. to a gendered title so as not to risk unemployment. HB1557 and its copycat laws express a position that LGBTQ+ people are lesser than their cisgender heterosexual counterparts, and are in fact, dangerous.

Anti-LGBTQ+ legislation has significant negative impacts on LGBTQ+ youth. These acts contribute to an atmosphere in which educators and staff may not support LGBTQ+ students in fear of violating the law. Nolan S. Kline and Stacey B. Griner note that HB1557 and copycat laws are, "messages of exclusion, which give rise to additional societal stressors and amplify existing stressors by instilling a sense of shame around one's own sexual orientation and gender identity."[31] The increased marginalization and stigmatization of LGBTQ+ populations and in particular LGBTQ+ youth lead to a heightening to risk for depression, self-harm, and suicide. Once rights-bearing creatures no longer have rights, or have those rights challenged, what is being challenged is our very personhood.

The changes and challenges to rights and freedoms, such as reproductive freedom or the freedom to express one's gender and sexuality among others we will discuss, are illustrative of the problem with relying upon liberalism. It is always possible to have one's rights, and thus one's personhood, stripped away. This has happened throughout the history of the United States, whether it be in terms of *Buck v. Bell*, where the State affirmed the power of individual states to sterilize disabled people and thus take away their right to reproductive freedom, or to reproductive freedom from those deemed "unfit" to procreate, framing it as a necessary measure to protect societal progress. In doing so, the State codified the idea that certain bodies—disabled bodies in this case—were less worthy of autonomy, citizenship, and inclusion within the liberal framework of personhood. The logic underpinning *Buck v. Bell* is not isolated but part of a broader historical pattern in which the State has used law to determine whose bodies and identities are valued and whose are expendable. This renegotiation of personhood continues to shape contemporary legal and political struggles. For example, anti-abortion laws, such as those spurred by *Dobbs v. Jackson Women's Health Organization*, similarly frame certain individuals—pregnant people in this case—as subordinate to State interests, stripping them of bodily autonomy under the pretense of protecting potential life. Within these cases, we see the State renegotiating whose bodies are more clearly aligned to liberal conception of personhood.

Rights are only worthwhile insofar as all human beings have them, and yet, these rights only matter insofar as they are recognized. Although disabled people, such as ourselves, have rights due to the 1990 American with Disabilities Act, many disabled people struggle to have those rights recognized and met. On March 21, 2023, a case was brought to the Supreme Court due to a child being denied their reasonable accommodations. *Perez v. Sturgis Public Schools.* Perez, a deaf child, was denied accommodations which included a sign-language interpreter. Perez sued under the ADA and Individuals with Disabilities Education Act (IDEA).[32] If we are rights-bearing creatures, then we are ultimately dependent upon the State to both recognize us as worthy of rights and to enforce those rights.

Liberalism has sought to address these problems. John Rawls was deeply concerned with inequality and how liberalism could possibly address it through distributive justice. Due to luck, some people will be born with more privilege and more opportunities than others. It is necessary that society redistributes goods in such a way that improves the lives of the least advantaged. Importantly, these structures would be set up institutionally *after* the Rawlsian system of justice has been established.[33] However, these institutions are not immediately focused upon the needs of those who experience significant disadvantages. It is unclear whether disadvantages due to physical or mental impairment, for example, would be considered in the originating principles of justice. Moreover, as Samuel Freeman argues:

> ...Rawls' difference principle is chosen by the parties in the original position for an ideal well-ordered society where everyone accepts the same principles of justice and these principles are fully enacted into law. But in non-ideal circumstances that do not comply with the difference principle, such as a capitalist society with huge inequalities...the application of the difference principle is not as straightforward.[34]

Rawls and Ronald Dworkin, each try to minimize and neutralize the deleterious effects of social class and natural talents, and in doing so appeal to social cooperation. However, for figures such as Martha Nussbaum and Amartya Sen, these appeals do not respond to the essential problem for liberalism—that justice may necessitate a reimagining of the liberal tradition through commitments.[35]

Nussbaum and Sen developed the capability approach, differing from a Rawlsian "primary good," to address this need for a reimagination. The capability approach guarantees a person ought to be able to carry out a capability, such as play, rather than providing an individual the thing related to the capability itself. Capabilities are expansive "in order to make room for choices."[36] According to Nussbuam and Sen, a society has an obligation to provide citizens with certain goods to flourish so that they may live a full life. Nussbaum establishes capabilities through a study of literature, particularly novels and argues that within novels we can understand a larger picture of what it means to be human, and that these works contribute to public reasoning. In *Poetic Justice*, Nussbaum states that she and Sen used Dickens' *Hard Times* in their analysis and critique of economic programs that study quality of life.[37] The practice of reading novels to learn more about the human condition is important. However, as Ebner-Landy notes, this approach also has the possibility of leading to the "creation of stereotypes by encouraging readers to develop ideas about people who seem to be in nominally similar situations to characters depicted in novels but, in fact, are not."[38] Ebner-Landy points out that this was Baldwin's critique of *Native Son*; additionally, "it is certainly possible that a marginalized person may not want to be seen with compassion but with respect, admiration, or even neutrality."[39] If we garner our conceptions of people solely through art, we run the risk of "dreaming" other people, and possibly romanticizing different struggles and oppressions we do not understand. While Nussbaum and Sen's capabilities approach is a marked shift in liberalism, and does present opportunities for linkages with our project, it has its own shortcomings with respect to addressing problems that may require intergenerational responsibility and considering obligations beyond ourselves.

The liberal conception of personhood and the language of rights prioritizes specific bodies and citizens. As Hyde explains, "bodies and indeed other people can be made to disappear in rights talk, their human attributes wrested from them and metaphorically assigned to imaginary, invasive, authoritarian state."[40] We hope within this book to illustrate an argument that liberalism is a coercive political philosophy which cannot meet human need and vulnerabilities. In light of that, we must utilize a theory of care. Care is an essential part of our lives, something that is an inescapable fact of Being. The current visibility of the law has been a way to penalize and regulate certain bodies. As explained by Mia Fischer, while visibility can be "seen as a measure of cultural justice and social equality" it also can "produce a pathway to biopolitical management, promoting techniques of surveillance, self-monitoring, self-responsibility for marginalized communities."[41] Within a theory of care, bodies are visible as sites of vulnerability, rather than sites of pathology. Moreover, it draws attention to our needs. It is a practice of an embodied political ethic, not of an esoteric discourse of rights, dependent upon the State to reify these rights. Rather, it is a consideration and a theory of vulnerability and fragility. A language of disability, gender, sexuality, and abortion that is not grounded in our embodied realities as beings with very real needs occludes a full consideration of our Being.

Expressing the Law

The question throughout this book is how we ought to understand the role of care in the law? Care is both a practice and an orientation toward an Other, or perhaps more appropriately for this project, our neighbor. Care ethics argues we exist in community with others; we are not free from our obligations. Likewise, the State is not free from its citizens. The State and the people who make up the body politic are interdependent. Rather than the liberal framework in which the State's role is minor, and the citizens are understood as rational, autonomous, and independent actors, care ethics imagines society as a matrix of inescapable relationships. These relationships may be distant. We may not know the students who attend the schools our taxes fund, but even so, we have an obligation to those public institutions. Ultimately, we are bound to one another, even if those relationships are unclear. We exist in a radical state of interdependence, and we can assess our immediate communities and to the State by our/its attentiveness to one another's needs.

The strong interpretation of the legal expressive theory is that law ought to be interpreted as expressions of the State's priorities. If the State does not, for example, ensure that people with disabilities are able to access measures to vote, then that lack of access would express a perspective that people with disabilities are not considered as full citizens. Likewise, if people who can become pregnant find themselves restricted to abortions based on the possibility the fetus would develop into a disabled child, as was the case in England and Wales' Abortion Act of 1967 which allowed exceptions to default positions on abortion regulations so long as there is a "substantial risk" that the child will be "seriously handicapped."[42]

Laws such as these are coercive. They promote a specific idea of personhood and limit pregnant people's options, placing them in a position in which their options are limited. This is particularly dire in the United States, as our social services are increasingly slashed for the prioritization of economic profit. The liberal actor does not need these social services, and it is western liberalism which emphasizes rationality, independence, and a choice-oriented actor, rather than a community or Other-oriented actor. Ultimately, if we seek to grapple with the problems of liberalism, it is essential to examine the law as a coercive expressive State apparatus.

The law operates both as a product of human agency—crafted through social, political, and cultural negotiations—and as an active force that shapes the fabric of society. It influences individual bodies and identities while constructing the collective makeup of entire nations, functioning as a framework for power and identity codification.[43] As Foucault suggests in *Discipline and Punish*, the "political technology of the body" aimed to produce "docile bodies," obscuring its normative framework through practices like internment, thereby giving rise to disciplinary institutions.[44] This dual role of law as both reactive and generative highlights its capacity to construct categories of race, gender, sexuality, and ability, reinforcing hierarchies of power and privilege.[45] "Law operates as a determinate, clearly bounded power that 'lays down a rule which demarcates the licit from the illicit, seeking to repress and negate that which it prohibits," Golder and Fitzpatrick explain.[46] It serves as a mechanism to normalize social and familial structures that align with State-sanctioned ideals, which in turn uphold capitalist frameworks reliant on specific configurations of labor, reproduction, and economic dependency.[47]

The law does not merely regulate bodies and sexualities through enforced compliance; rather, it actively produces them. As Butler explains, the subject is shaped by a "set of actions mobilized by the law," which in turn "produces material effects."[48] By reconsidering how the law construct, and is constructed by "embodiment, responsibility, and obedience," one can better understand how the law itself inscribes bodies with meaning.[49] "[T]he body of the law also created more specific bodies, the regulation of which serves the substantive political and legal disciplinary function of manning a specific social order," Cheah, Fraser, and Grbich assert.[50] Pathologization is one such method of enforcing social orders.

Pathologization operates as a tool for legal and social control, constructing deviance as both a moral and medicalized category to justify exclusion and surveillance (See *Discipline and Punishment* and the *History of Sexuality*). "These legal subjects are thus incorporated into a limited juridical status which defines them, by inclusion, exclusion, or extermination from the body politic," Cheah, Fraser, and Grbich explain.[51] Anti-abortion and anti-sodomy laws are prominent examples of this dynamic, portraying certain bodies and behaviors as incompatible with State-sanctioned morality.[52] These laws enforce cisnormativity and heteronormativity, ensuring bodies conform to roles that sustain capitalist productivity and social hierarchy.[53] This pathologization not only marginalizes individuals but actively constructs deviant categories to maintain systems of power. As queer legal theorists emphasize, legal frameworks do not merely reflect societal norms but actively participate in producing and regulating categories of deviance, sexuality, and embodiment.[54]

The regulation of sexual behavior and reproduction is deeply tied to broader efforts to uphold patriarchal and capitalist systems. Laws governing contraception and abortion pathologize reproductive autonomy by framing it as a threat to social stability. The roots of this regulation are visible in the legacy of Comstock-era laws, which sought to suppress non-procreative sexual behavior under the guise of public morality.[55] This historical lineage reflects how law weaponizes morality to justify control over bodies and behaviors. Anti-contraception advocates, for instance, continue to rely on pseudoscientific claims about the harm of contraception to women, masking their broader opposition to non-procreative sex.[56] Similarly, contemporary anti-abortion laws pathologize the exercise of reproductive autonomy, framing it as morally and socially dangerous.

The legal construction of deviance has also historically shaped the regulation of LGBTQ+ identities. In the late nineteenth and early twentieth centuries, laws against cross-dressing, sodomy, and "obscenity" and "perversity" were central to criminalizing same-sex intimacy, regulating immigration, and enforcing heteronormative ideals.[57] As explained by Margot Canady, in the early 1900s, "Federal officials...worried about those whose bodies or behaviors seemed perverse to them." By the mid-1940s and later, the "state crafted tools to overtly target homosexuality."[58]

These laws not only marginalized queer people but also created the category of the "homosexual" as a deviant figure, subject to surveillance and exclusion. As Canady argues, the State itself constructed the "homosexual" by categorizing "certain sexual behaviors, gender traits, and emotional ties as grounds for exclusion."[59] Legal systems, through their regulatory frameworks, produce boundaries of acceptability while relegating those who resist or challenge dominant norms to the margins.[60] Therefore, Canady argues, "homosexuality is thus a legal category."[61]

Nussbaum's theory of disgust and shame are particularly salient in this regard. Nussbaum argues that disgust and shame are two strong emotions we see within law, each holding specific dangers. Disgust "imputes to the object properties that make it no longer a member of the subject's own community or world, a kind of alien species of thing."[62] Shame operates somewhat differently, referring to a "sense of failure to attain some ideal state."[63] LGBTQ+ people and people with disabilities are frequently the site of both emotions.

Disgust turns queer people into villains and threats against the family and community, and people with disabilities are asked to hide their disabilities so as to comfort the abled—Nussbaum looks at the example of blind people wearing sunglasses for the comfort of sighted people.[64] Shame, through stigma and classifications of people as "others," denies the fact that we have a shared humanity. Furthermore, these classifications invite the public to reinforce shame. Nussbaum argues that queer people and people with disabilities are on the receiving end of these emotions because we are disruptive. The public existence of people with disabilities reminds "normals," to use Nussbaum's language, that they too have vulnerable bodies. The public existence of queer people causes a type of anxiety, because they are seen as symbols of sexuality and gender; moreover, they are seen as examples of change. Due to this, their existence is a threat to "normalcy."

These two emotions lead to the development of two worlds—"the public world of the ordinary citizen and the hidden world…."[65] This hidden world is the world of deviants, and Nussbaum focuses particularly on people with disabilities. However, with the advent of "Don't Say Gay Laws," LGBTQ+ people are increasingly becoming a part of this hidden world. This hiding away of people with disabilities and LGBTQ+ people emerges from shame's drive to cordon off the impaired and imperfect.

These efforts represent, according to Judith Butler and particularly in terms of gender identity and queerness, the power of critique. Gender has become seen as such a threat that it is mobilizing global responses to limit and define its expressions and identities. Butler writes, "[w]ith critique comes a new way of understanding the world, one that can be essential to struggles for social change and the opening up of new possible ways of living."[66] Critique of gender does not undo categories of "women" and "men," but rather opens us up to imagining other ways of expressing, recognizing, and identifying ourselves. Queerness gives all people access to a form of freedom that is seen as "excessive" by the far-right and thus must be legally restrained.

Queer legal theory provides critical insight into how the law's regulatory functions extend beyond passive reflection of societal norms to active participation in the construction of deviance and conformity. The trajectory of LGBTQ+ rights in the United States exemplifies the paradox of legal recognition and inclusion.

Visibility itself, as Foucault observed, becomes a tool of discipline.[67] Legal reforms frequently construct marginalized identities as subjects of protection while simultaneously subjecting them to heightened regulation and surveillance.[68] For example, while Title IX offered protections for transgender individuals, those coexisted with increasing legislative attacks on transgender rights, reinforcing their precarious position within the social order.[69] Similarly, contemporary laws targeting LGBTQ+ education, such as Florida's "Don't Say Gay" laws, exemplify how the State uses silence and exclusion to regulate queer visibility while fostering hostile environments that exacerbate marginalization and harm.[70] This duality underscores the precariousness of legal recognition, which frequently operates within frameworks that simultaneously include and marginalize.[71]

Both anti-transgender legislation and anti-abortion laws weaponize notions of pathology and deviance, framing their targets as dangers to societal stability. These laws rely on morality and discipline to reinforce a biopolitical order where certain bodies are deemed productive and normative while others are excluded or expendable.[72] The interplay between inclusion and marginalization highlights the law's role in constructing and regulating deviant bodies to sustain systems of power.[73] Queer legal theory reveals that these regulatory functions are not incidental but central to the operation of legal systems. By constructing deviance, the law actively maintains its normative frameworks, creating a landscape in which certain lives and bodies are deemed valuable and legitimate while others are pathologized and excluded.[74] Visibility, rather than inherently liberating, often disciplines, obliging bodies to conform to the State's goals of optimization and control.[75] Thus, the law's gaze remains deeply invested in upholding systems of power that rely on exclusion and marginalization to sustain themselves.[76]

Combining our theoretical analysis with a critical disabilities approach, our first chapter focuses on disability within the United States. A critical disability studies framework of legal embodiment focuses on how sociopolitical and physical topographies are accessed or not accessed by people with disabilities at varying times and in varying spaces. People with disabilities experience significant challenges to access anti-discrimination law. The Civil Rights Act of 1964 does not include disability as a protected class. Due to this, Section 504 of the Rehabilitation Act of 1973 and Americans with Disabilities Act of 1990 are used to hold institutions, particularly educational institutions, to account for accommodations.[77] People with disabilities are held to a differing standard from other identities due to the demands of medical evidence of their needs. As Section 504 is challenged in the Supreme Court in the case *A.J.T. v. Osseo Area Schools*, the subject of legal embodiment for people with disabilities is a critical question. Our analytical framework promotes a disability forward framework for engagement with the law and contends that hyper-visibility ought to be used by people with disabilities to foreground their experiences. We draw largely on Valentine's experiences within the medical system, using a hybrid autoethnographical approach to provide insight into the US system of disabilities.

Autoethnography as a discipline emerges from sociology and has focused on social structures. Arthur Bochner describes its purpose as making "social science something more than an end in itself."[78] In the context of this book, and in particular our first chapter, it renders our theories concrete. Within disability studies, much work has been done in the scope of emancipatory research that empowers people with disabilities through utilizing the researchers' expertise to further the goals and perspectives of people with disabilities.[79] Autoethnography, for us, is a method in which the author offers themselves and their experience to the reader, and in light of this, invites the reader to know Valentine and hopefully further understand their perspective and critique.

The Western liberal tradition asserts the normative body as white, cisgender, heterosexual, masculine, and able-bodied among other significant identities. To be a person with disabilities is to exist outside of this tradition, and thus one is forcibly made known and disclosed through their disability. Some bodies and some disabilities may be more visible than others. Others, such as Valentine's diagnosis of epilepsy, may be hyper-visible for a moment before retreating to invisibility. To be known in a legal context within the United States has a fraught history for people with disabilities, particularly with precedents such as *Buck v. Bell* which provides states with the right to sterilize people with disabilities. If the law expresses the perspectives of the State, as we contend it does, then we must attend to the ways in which disability laws continue to prioritize a Western liberal tradition, thereby unable to fully understand people with disabilities as political actors in their own right.

Chapter 3 examines public education, which has become an increasingly salient realm of contesting political and legislative perspectives on gender and sexuality. DeSantis' "Don't Say Gay" Bill initiated a series of nationwide anti-LGBTQ+ legislation. The bill, and its copycats, outlaws any discussions of gender or sexuality with students. Parents may file complaints if they suspect the law is in violation. As a result, educators have found their ability to support and care for students to be limited so as to avoid felony charges of violating the bill. Educators who are LGBTQ+ have also found themselves silenced. Transgender educators have been penalized for using titles and pronouns that reflect their gender identity. Although LGBTQ+ people are a protected class under Title IX, these acts hope to push LGBTQ+ people out of public spaces like education and are right-wing attacks on expressions of gender and sexuality which do not align with right-wing cisheterosexual patriarchal Judeo-Christian values.

The contemporary pushback against LGBTQ+ people in the United States has gained popularity alongside restrictions on abortion and reproductive rights, which utilize similar logistics as anti-LGBTQ+ legislation. Both are attempts to legislate and regulate specific forms of sexuality, and assert a normative perspective that is neoconversative. Conservatives, particularly evangelicals, had long been ambivalent on the question of abortion.[80] However, in the twenty-first century, neoconservatives and the religious right have contributed to anti-abortion legislation, which has had significant deleterious effects on the lives of pregnant people. States that have severely restricted abortions increased a 16% increase in infant mortality. Abortion restrictions also correlated with higher rates of maternal mortality.[81] The indications for abortion bans and restrictions are stark.

Pregnancy is in itself a unique experience, and the history of abortion access within the United States has frequently rested upon arguments of rights and personhood. Yet, the language of rights pits pregnant people's freedoms against those of the fetus, making abortion into a question of whose rights "win," rather than considering pregnancy and abortion as intimate relational experiences. This dialogue further stigmatizes people who pursue abortions. Within Chapter 4, we examine dialogue pre-during-after legislation of abortion restrictions in the United States, focusing in particular on the language of personhood and rights. Central to this discussion is the concept of the "obscene." Obscenity seems to convey more than a notion of something hidden or sexually explicit; it reflects a tool of power and control, which enables the shaping of bodies and behaviors through patterns of visibility and prohibition. In the case of abortion, its labeling as "obscene" then becomes a part of discipline by which reproductive autonomy has been depicted as deviant and hence bound under strict regulation. This dynamic is highlighted in the revival of the Comstock Act, which utilizes a broad definition of obscenity to impose a moral and legal framework—one that suppresses reproductive choices by making certain aspects of pregnancy and abortion unspeakable or taboo.

LGBTQ+ rights in the United States saw significant progress in the 2000s, followed by rapid regression in the 2020s. The *Dobbs* decision, which ended federal protections for abortion access, has been leveraged to undermine transgender healthcare rights. In 2023 alone, 87 anti-transgender laws were enacted, targeting education, healthcare, and library resources. Simultaneously, transgender individuals have been recognized under Title IX as a protected class against sex discrimination. This paradox positions transgender people as both threats to society and vulnerable populations in need of protection, reflecting a legal duality that is reminiscent of the historical criminalization of queer identities. Chapter 5 explores how bans on gender-affirming care and other legislative attacks maintain the long legacy of policing queer bodies and spaces. It contextualizes these policies within a history of systemic violence and control that reveals how such intersections—and the lived experiences of its authors—can sustain a legacy of exclusion, punishment, and enforced conformity.

We write this book in the aftermath of the US 2024 presidential election. Trump's win comes at a time when anti-LGBTQ+ legislation, attacks on education and reproductive rights have swept across the United States. The State, and in particular the Supreme Court, have articulated a legal vision of personhood that prioritizes cisgender, heterosexual, able-bodied, white, male, and upper to middle class people. The legislation that we examine in our book has made specific bodies visible, and that visibility has been used to penalize those bodies. *Dobbs* and other cases have contributed to an America where certain people's futures are uncertain or are directly limited.

Critically, our political landscape, in which self-titled progressives have looked away from transgressions on transgender people's rights, has been able to become so convoluted due to an important fact of liberalism—it is a theory of rights, not a theory of need. Liberalism is unable to meet our needs, because it is based upon the idea of the rational self-interested individual, rather than human beings as fragile vulnerable creatures. That political actor has no needs that they cannot meet themselves. Why should we expect its language to be different? If we have no language of need or of frailty, then it would seem we cannot escape the problems of liberalism. However, we do have a language of need. We find that language in care ethics, in human fragility. Ultimately, the response to a State whose legislation expresses a perspective in which marginalized minorities are not prioritized is not to seek refuge in liberalism's promises of rights and freedoms *from* abuse or want. Rather, it necessitates a re-Orientation toward one another. Our obligations exist before and after us. It is in these obligations and our radical lack of freedom that we will find our refuge.

Jonathan Herring describes care as, "the most primary value as it is essential to meet people's most basic survival needs, without that talk of justice would be meaningless. We need to support and enable care, so that justice can be considered. To be blunt we could survive in a society which was not just, but we could not survive in a society in which there is no care."[82] The contemporary assaults on the dignity of marginalized persons are also assaults on justice through their undermining of care. For this reason, any legal challenge to the Trump administration, or the global far-right, must prioritize care. If we fail to do so, then marginalized people become accepted human collateral.

It is undeniable that law can act as a tool for progress. In response to *Dobbs*, many judges attempted to impede trigger bans in states such as Louisiana and Texas. Likewise the disability frame of law, which is used to frame particular problems as concerning disability, has been used to protect people with disabilities.[83] Similarly, it has been used to address and bolster environmental protections as ways to protect people with asthma and to mitigate the disabling effects of pollution.[84] We do not intend for this work to argue *against* legal intervention, but to argue that the law in and of itself cannot preserve human dignity because it is constructed to violently uphold State power. Particularly as challenges to previously established protections for transgender people, people with disabilities, and people who can be pregnant among other groups proliferate the American political system and courts. Rather, it is a question of our social life and ultimately of political ethics. Within this, we may find a voice in Simone Weil, who in her critique of liberalism suggested that we look to human being as that which is essential:

> at the bottom of the heart of every human being, from earliest infancy until the tomb, there is something that goes on indomitably expecting, in the teeth all experience of crimes committed, suffered, and witnessed, that good and not evil will be done to him. It is this above all that is sacred in every human being...a political party busily seeking, or maintaining itself in power can discern nothing in these cries except a noise...it can never be capable of the tender and sensitive attention which is needed to understand its meaning.[85]

We will not find the preservation of our dignity in a political party. Instead, we must cultivate a political ethic of care which asks us to attend toward concrete responsibilities and obligations we have toward one another and to the future. This will require a dialectic of care, in which we all provide and receive care, and within this we can pursue varying strategies without relying solely upon rights-based approaches.

Notes

1. Michel de Certeatu, *The Practice of Everyday Life*, Translated by Steven Rendall (Berkeley: University of California Press, 1984), 139–140.
2. Alan Hyde, *Bodies of Law*, (Princeton: Princeton University Press, 2001), 8.
3. Wendy Brown, *State of Injury: Power and Freedom in Late Modernity* (Princeton: Princeton University Press, 1995), 174.
4. Ibid., 9.
5. Pheng Cheah, David Fraser & Judith Grbich, *Thinking Through the Body of the Law* (New York: NYU Press, 1996), xi.
6. Ibid., xii.

7. Adrienne Rich, "Politics of Location," *in Sexy Bodies: The Strange Carnalities of Feminism*, eds. Elizabeth Grosz and Elspeth Probyn (Psychology Press, 1995), 215.
8. Pheng Cheah, David Fraser and Judith Grbich, *Thinking Through the Body of the Law*, xii.
9. Ibid., xii–xiv.
10. Heloise Robinson, "Prenatal Testing, Disability Equality, and the Limits of the Law," *The New Bioethics* 29, no.3(2023): 203; Erik Parens and Adrienne Asch, "Special Supplement: The Disability Rights Critique of Prenatal Genetic Testing Reflections and Recommendations," *The Hastings Center Report* 29, no.5(1999): S1–S2; Hans S. Reinders, *The Future of the Disabled in a Liberal Society: An Ethical Analysis* (University of Notre Dame Press, 2009).
11. Adrienne Rich, "Politics of Location," 215.
12. *Norwegian and American Laws* (De Gruyter Open Press, 2014,) 1.
13. Michel Foucault, *Discipline and Punish: The Birth of the Prison* (New York: Vintage Books, 1995), 200.
14. Ibid.
15. Achille Mbembe, "Necropolitics," *Public Culture* 15, no. 1 (2003): 12.
16. Mia Fischer, *Terrorizing Gender: Transgender Visibility and the Surveillance Practices of the U.S. Security State* (Lincoln: University of Nebraska Press, 2019), 170.
17. Carly Thomsen, *Visibility Interrupted: Rural Queer Life and the Politics of Unbecoming* (University of Minnesota Press, 2021); Michel Foucault, *Discipline and Punish.*
18. Andrea Mubi Brighenti, *Visibility in Social Theory and Social Research* (Palgrave McMillan, 2010), 48.
19. Rachel Adams, "Choosing Disability, Visualizing Care," *Kennedy Institute of Ethics Journal* 27, no.2(2017); Jenny Morris, "Care or Empowerment? A Disability Rights Perspective," *Social Policy and Administration* 31, no.1(1997): 54–60; Gillian Parker and Harriet Clarke, "Making the Ends Meet: Do Carers and Disabled People Have a Common Agenda?" *Policy & Politics* 30, no.3(2002): 347–359; Teppo Kröger, "Care Research and Disability Studies: Nothing in Common?" *Critical Social Policy* 29, no.3(2009): 404.

20. "Declaration of Independence," *America's Founding Documents*, https://www.archives.gov/founding-docs/declaration-transcript.
21. Jamal Greene, *How Rights Wen Wrong: Why Our Obsession with Rights Is Tearing America Apart* (Boston: Houghton Mifflin Harcout, 2021), 32.
22. Ibid., 56.
23. Ibid., 8.
24. Supreme Court of the United States, "Gonzalez v. Carhart," 2007, https://supreme.justia.com/cases/federal/us/550/124/.
25. Riley Clare Valentine, "Who has a meaningful life? A care ethics analysis of selective trait abortion," *Medicine, Health Care and Philosophy* (2024): 1–12.
26. Adrienne Asch, "Prenatal Diagnosis and Selective Abortion: A Challenge to Practice and Policy," *American Journal of Public Health* 89, no.11(1999): 1652.
27. Hans S. Reinders, *The Future of the Disabled in a Liberal Society*, 182; Chris Kaposy, "A Disability Critique of the New Prenatal Test for Down Syndrome," *Kennedy Institute of Ethics* Journal 23, no.4(2013): 299–324.
28. Eva Feder Kittay and Leo Kittay, "On the Expressivity and Ethics of Selective Abortion for Disability: Conversations with My Son," In *Norms and Values: Essays on the Work of Virginia Held* (Rowman & Littlefield, 1998).
29. Abbie E. Goldberg, "Impact of HB 1557 (Florida's Don't Say Gay Bill) on LGBTQ+ Parents in Florida," *UCLA School of Law Williams Institute,* January 2023, https://williamsinstitute.law.ucla.edu/wp-content/uploads/Dont-Say-Gay-Impact-Jan-2023.pdf.
30. "Parental Rights in Education," HB 1557, 2022, https://www.flsenate.gov/Session/Bill/2022/1557.
31. Nolan S. Kline, Stacey B. Griner, Malinee Neelamegam, Nathaniel J. Webb, Joél Junior Morales, and Scott D. Rhodes, "Responding to 'Don't Say Gay' Laws in the US: Research Priorities and Considerations for Health Equity," *Sex Res Social Policy* 19, no.4(2022): 1398.
32. Supreme Court of the United States, "Luna Perez v. Sturgis Public Schools et al.," 2022, https://www.supremecourt.gov/opinions/22pdf/21-887_k53m.pdf.

33. John Rawls, *Justice as Fairness: A Restatement* (Cambrigde: Harvard University Press, 2001); John Rawls, *A Theory of Justice* (Cambrigde: Belknap Press, 1999).
34. Samuel Freeman, "Liberalism and Distributive Justice: A Prècis," *Philosophy and Public Issues (New Series)* 10, no.1(2020): 12.
35. Martha Nussbaum, *Creating Capabilities: The Human Development Approach* (Cambridge: Belknap Press, 2011); Amartya Sen, *The Idea of Justice* (Cambridge: Belknap Press, 2009).
36. Martha Nussbaum, *Creating Capabilities*, xix.
37. Martha Nussbaum, *Poetic Justice: The Literary Imagination and Public Life* (Boston: Beacon Press, 1996), xv–xvi.
38. Katie Ebner-Landy, "A Critique of Martha Nussbuam's Liberal Aesthetics," *Political Theory* 52, no.2(2024): 23.
39. Ibid.
40. Alan Hyde, *Bodies of Law*, 264.
41. Mia Fischer, *Terrorizing Gender*, 14.
42. Hans S. Reinders, *The Future of the Disabled in a Liberal Society.*
43. Ian Haney López, *White by Law: The Legal Construction of Race,* (New York: NYU Press, 2006), 3.
44. Michel Foucault, *Discipline and Punish,* 200.
45. Ashley E. McGovern, "When Schools Refuse to 'Say Gay': The Constitutionality of Anti-LGBTQ 'No-Promo-Homo' Public School Policies in the United States," *Cornell Journal of Law and Public Policy* 22 (2012): 465–467.
46. Ben Golder and Peter Fitzpatrick, *Foucault's Law* (Routledge-Cavendish, 2009).
47. Blanca L. Hernandez, "The Prurient Investment: How First Amendment Speech Jurisprudence Obstructs the Movement for LGBT Equality," *Southern California Review of Law and Social Justice* 22 (2013): 380–382.
48. Judith Butler, *Bodies That Matter: On the Discursive Limits of Sex* (New York: Routledge, 1993), xxii.
49. Pheng Cheah, David Fraser & Judith Grbich, *Thinking Through the Body of the Law*, xv–xvii.
50. Ibid., xii.
51. Ibid., xvii.
52. Robin Maril, "Queer Rights After *Dobbs v. Jackson Women's Health Organization*," *San Diego Law Review* 60 (2023): 46.
53. Ibid., 51–52.

54. Hunter Foist, "Keep Saying Gay: How Nationwide 'Don't Say Gay' Bills Violate the First Amendment, Chill Protected Speech, and Hinder Public Health Outcomes," *Indiana Health Law Review* 21 (2024): 177–178.
55. Priscilla J. Smith, "Contraceptive Comstockery: Reasoning from Immorality to Illness in the Twenty-First Century," *Connecticut Law Review* 47 (2015): 974.
56. Ibid.
57. William N. Eskridge Jr. "Law and the Construction of the Closet: American Regulation of Same-Sex Intimacy, 1880–1946," *Iowa Law Review* 82 (1997): 1009.
58. Margot Canady, *The Straight State: Sexuality and Citizenship in Twentieth-Century America* (Princeton: Princeton University Press, 2009), 3.
59. Ibid., 4.
60. Hunter Foist, "Keep Saying Gay," 177–178.
61. Ibid.
62. Martha Nussbaum, *Hiding From Humanity: Disgust, Shame, and the Law* (Princeton: Princeton University Press, 2004), 166.
63. Ibid., 184.
64. Ibid., 293.
65. Ibid., 308.
66. Judith Butler, *Who's Afraid of Gender?* (New York: Farrar, Straus and Giroux, 2024), 141.
67. Michel Foucault, *Discipline and Punish*, 210.
68. Laura Beth Nielsen, Elsinore Kuo, and Evan Zhao, "Misgendering, Academic Freedom, and Trans Students," *Case Western Reserve Law Review* 73 (2023): 1179.
69. National Center for Transgender Equality, "New Title IX Rules Protect Our Trans Students", April 19, 2024, https://transequality.org/news/new-title-ix-rules-protect-our-trans-students; Zane McNeill, "93% of Trans Teens Live in States That Have Proposed or Passed Anti-Trans Laws", TRUTHOUT (April 15, 2024), https://truthout.org/articles/93-of-trans-teens-live-in-states-that-have-proposed-or-passed-anti-trans-laws/.
70. Clifford Rosky, "Don't Say Gay: The Government's Silence and the Equal Protection Clause," *University of Illinois Law Review* (2022): 1849.
71. Hunter Foist, "Keep Saying Gay," 185.

72. June Carbone, and Naomi Cahn, "The Court's Morality Play: The Punishment Lens, Sex, and Abortion," *Southern California Law Review* 96 (2023): 1105–6.
73. Ibid.
74. Michel Foucault, *Discipline and Punish*, 213.
75. Ibid.
76. Blanca L. Hernandez, "The Prurient Investment," 401.
77. Lauren Shallish, "'Just How Much Diversity Will the Law Permit?': The Americans with Disabilities Act, Diversity, and Disability in Higher Education," *Disability Studies Quarterly* 35,no.3(2015).
78. Arthur Bochner and Carolyn Ellis, "Why Autoethnography?" *Social Work and Social Sciences Review* 23, no.2(2022): 8–18; Carolyn Ellis, Tony E. Adams, and Arthur P. Bochner, "Autoethnography: An Overview," *Historical Social Research/ Historische Sozialforschung* (2011): 273–290.
79. Amy J. Peterson, "Research with Individuals Labeled 'Other': Reflections on the Research Process," *Disability & Society* 26, no.3(2011): 293–305; Len Barton, "Emancipatory Research and Disabled People: Some Observations and Questions," *Educational Review* 57, no.3(2005): 317–327; Mike Oliver, "Emancipatory Research: Realistic Goal or Impossible Dream?" *Doing Disability Research* 2(1997): 15–31; Jenny Morris, "Personal and Political: A Feminist Perspective on Researching Physical Disability," *Disability, Handicap & Society* 7, no.2(1992): 157–167.
80. Melinda Cooper, *Family Values: Between Neoliberalism and the New Social Conservatism* (New York: Zone Books, 2021).
81. Kendall J. Burdick et al., "Abortion Restrictiveness and Infant Mortality: An Ecologic Study," *Americal Journal of Preventative Medicine* 66,no.3(2024): 418–426; Pabayo R, Ehntholt A, Cook DM, Reynolds M, Muennig P, Liu SY, "Laws Restricting Access to Abortion Services and Infant Mortality Risk in the United States," *International Journal of Environmental Research and Public Health* 17, no.11(2020): 3773; Eugene Declercq et al., "The U.S. Maternal Health Divide: The limited maternal health services and worse outcomes of states proposing new abortion restrictions Abortion Restrictions Affect Mortality Ratel," *Commonwealth Fund*, https://www.commonwealthfund.org/publications/issue-briefs/2022/dec/us-maternal-health-divide-limited-services-worse-outcomes.

82. Jonathan Herring, *Caring and the Law* (Portland, Oregon: Hart Publishing, 2013), 41.
83. Jasmine E. Harris and Karen M. Tani, "The Disability Frame," *University of Pennsylvania Law Review* 170, no.7(2022): 1164.
84. Ibid., 1677.
85. Simone Weil, "Human Personality," in *Simone Weil: An Anthology*, ed. Siân Miles, London: Virago (1986): 50, 53.

CHAPTER 2

Disability, Valentine's Narrative, and the Law

Abstract Some bodies are unknown. They understood as being *the* body upon which law comes from, and in the Western liberal tradition that normative body is white, cisgender, heterosexual, able-bodied, and male, among other significant identities. To be a person with disabilities is then to be forcibly made known and disclosed. Some bodies and some disabilities can make a person who may be ordinarily materially anonymous, hyper-visible for a moment, and that visibility will recede until the person is again made anonymous. Nonetheless, at various times episodic disabilities such as epilepsy have been rendered highly visible. A critical disability studies framework of legal embodiment focuses on how sociopolitical and physical topographies are accessed or not accessed by people with disabilities at varying times and in varying spaces. Such a framework prioritizes these variations, for multiple reasons. One being that as technologies increase, people with disabilities may be able to involve themselves in aspects of life which were previously inaccessible. The second is that individuals whose bodies are liminally visible may experience restrictions to these topographies in a unique fashion which is contingent on the episodic nature of their disability. This analytical framework promotes a disability forward framework for engagement with the law and contends that hyper-visibility ought to be used by people with disabilities to foreground their experiences.

R. C. Valentine and Z. McNeill, *The Coercive Power of the Law*,
https://doi.org/10.1007/978-3-032-07589-5_2

Keywords Normative body · Disability · Personhood · Material anonymity · Visibility

Material anonymity is a theory of legal embodiment which contends certain bodies are rendered anonymous due to their assumption of being normativewhite, cisgender, heterosexual, able-bodied, and male, among other categories.[1] To be a person with disabilities is then, to be forcibly made known and disclosed. However, some disabilities are sporadically made visible, troubling a binary understanding of embodiment. Some bodies and some disabilities can make a person who may be ordinarily materially anonymous, hyper-visible for a moment, and that visibility will recede until the person is again made anonymous. Nonetheless, at various times episodic disabilities such as epilepsy have been rendered highly visible, such as in the case *Buck v. Bell*. The Supreme Court in the 1927 case *Buck v. Bell* upheld the right of individual states to forcibly sterilize people, primarily women, who were epileptic, bipolar, or schizophrenic. Carrie Buck was a poor white woman, diagnosed as "feeble minded" who did not want to be sterilized, and she lost that battle.[2] Bodies that are sometimes visible and other times do not occupy a liminal space.

This unevenness illustrates the performative power of law in constructing disability as a category of exclusion and control. The legal system functions not as a neutral framework but as a producer of embodied hierarchies. Disability becomes a marker of deviance and disposability, enabling the State and its institutions to regulate bodies under the guise of order, safety, and societal stability. Foucault's concept of the "political technology of the body" highlights how law, medicine, and social norms converge to delineate bodies as productive or unproductive, worthy or unworthy.[3] These categorizations are not neutral but deeply embedded in racialized, gendered, and colonial logics, operating to sustain systems of exploitation and marginalization.

Disability provides us, as Nancy J. Hirschmann writes with "intersectionality with intersectionality."[4] Roughly 13.6% of Americans have a disability, and the majority of those people develop their disabilities later in life.[5] Any person can become disabled. Intersectionality is frequently used within feminist theory as a way of distinguishing oneself. Within the disability framework, it is a way of identifying similarity *through* difference. My experience as someone with epilepsy is not the same as someone with cerebral palsy. Nor is my experience the same as other people with epilepsy who may have a different form of epilepsy. Yet, we face significant overlaps when it comes to exclusion and marginalization on the basis of disability. The disability approach is akin to Carol Gilligan, the founder of care ethics, conception of "web" in which we are interconnected directly or indirectly.[6] These connections tie us to one another, and from a disability lens, asks that we critically examine the relationship of the State and people with disabilities.

Necropolitics further sharpens this analysis by exposing the State's role in determining which lives are preserved and which are rendered expendable. Disability, through legal embodiment, becomes a key site of this necropolitical calculus. The bodies labeled as disabled are often subjected to conditions of slow death—whether through structural abandonment, poverty, or exclusion from healthcare and public life—under the pretense of medical or legal necessity. This necropolitical dynamic underscores how the labeling of disability is not merely about classification but about the deliberate exercise of sovereign power to decide life and death.

Moreover, the State's construction of disability serves to stabilize normative frameworks of ability, class, race, and gender, reinforcing the hierarchies upon which its governance depends. Law becomes the arbiter of who is allowed to thrive and who is left to wither, a mechanism that sustains neoliberal capitalism by categorizing bodies into hierarchies of value. Disability is thus revealed not as a static or universal condition but as a dynamic and contested site where the intersecting forces of law, power, and embodiment shape the contours of social life and death.

The law is not neutral nor is it silent in terms of disabilities, including liminal disabilities. Many states within the United States limit a person's ability to drive if they have a seizure and the timeline for which they are barred from driving may vary from State to State. These laws do not always distinguish between forms of seizures. Thus, a myoclonic jerk of a finger may result in the same penalty as that of a tonic clonic seizure; however, this is highly dependent upon how strictly the law is enforced, or upon a person's disclosure.

Many people are unaware that when I shudder, particularly if it begins in my shoulders, that they are witnessing a seizure. It is only the type of seizure for which I experience an "aura," a term used for the sensations a person may have before a seizure – an itching begins inside my brain, it feels as though there is an itch lying beneath my skull, and a tension and tremor uncurl from my shoulders up to my head.

If the law were to be aptly applied, it would require people to be highly trained and aware of the various forms of seizures people with epilepsy experience or require us to report each and every seizure.[7] Bodies with episodic disabilities are faced with direct consequences and held to heightened scrutiny in which they are expected to share details of their experiences in a way that may be unfathomable for other bodies. Bodies which are liminally visible due to these episodic disabilities are highly visible within the law. Moreover, they experience a significant form of visibility due to the element of forcible self-disclosure.

Legal embodiment is a theory of how institutions and discourses of law mediate various bodies. A critical disability studies framework of legal embodiment focuses on how sociopolitical and physical topographies are accessed or not accessed by people with disabilities at varying times and in varying spaces. Such a framework prioritizes these variations, for multiple reasons. One being that as technologies increase, people with disabilities may be able to involve themselves in aspects of life which were previously inaccessible. The second is that individuals whose bodies are liminally visible may experience restrictions to these topographies in a unique fashion which is contingent on the episodic nature of their disability. This analytical framework promotes a disability forward framework for engagement with the law and contends that hyper-visibility ought to be used by people with disabilities to foreground their experiences. Despite the usefulness of hyper-visibility, visibility within the law ought not to be interpreted as something positive, but rather as an expression of the State's perspective.

Afflicting the Public

In the late nineteenth century the United States implemented various forms of "ugly laws." These laws prohibited anything or anyone who could be upsetting, disturbing, or insulting from appearing in public. Simon Williams notes that any body that was seen as vulgar, dysfunctional, or in some way *other* was made into a "dys-appearing body."[8] Ugly laws disciplined not just the bodies who were disappeared by these laws but also the public; Susan Schweik writes "the public was also more directly disciplined, constituted as *that* which at all costs must not view *this*."[9] She cites a Portland ordinance which stated, "If any crippled, maimed or deformed person shall beg upon the streets or in any public place, they shall upon conviction thereof before the Police Court, be fined not less than five dollars nor more than one hundred dollars."[10] Portland was an outlier in its specific focus upon panhandling; the quality of physical impairment was what Schweik describes as "status offense," only being enforced if the person had no means. These laws draw, then, on both ableism and classism. It allowed for the public to banish the "unsightly beggar."[11] People with disabilities, both then and now, struggled to access the same economic opportunities as people without disabilities, and as a result had profound consequences for people with disabilities, particularly visible disabilities.

People with invisible disabilities, such as epilepsy, also experienced the label of "unsightliness." Schweik quotes Charles Henderson's 1906 account on what the public ought to do if they see a person having an epileptic seizure:

> In sociable intercourse the epileptic is an object of dread, and no one who has witnessed the person in a convulsion can quite escape from the haunting memory of the spectacle and entirely free his mind from terror or disgust. Hence there cannot be that free, unconstrained, and natural converse which gives pleasure to society.[12]

Schweik attends to Henderon's usage of "Hence there cannot be." Henderson appears to be claiming as a natural fact that people with epilepsy cannot be sociable, not only for ourselves, but also for the public. Our presence in public "constitutes it as perpetual horror."[13] Ugly laws ultimately sought to enforce cultural norms of politeness and seemliness, as Schweik writes—the laws legislated who *ought* to be self-regulated. The removal of people from public life highlighted whose bodies could be part of everyday society, and those whose bodies could not. The regulatory impacts of the ugly laws define specific bodies as deviant, and ultimately those bodies were frequently people with disabilities, BBIPOC (Black, brown, indigenous, and people of color) people, and women.

Disability was a broad category, and people could be *dis*-abled so as to justify their oppression or removal from public life. Douglas C. Baynton found that anti-suffragists argued women inherently had "disabilities that made them incapable of using the franchise responsibility, and that because of their frailty women would become disabled if exposed to the rigors of political participation."[14] Likewise, Black people in the United States were found to be disabled outside of slavery, "American blacks, for example, were said to flourish in their 'normal condition' of slavery, while the "free' or abnormal negro' inevitably fell into illness, disability, and eventually extinction."[15]

Disability is not merely a biological or medical condition but a legal and social construct shaped through the interplay of power, knowledge, and law. It is a category strategically deployed to delineate which bodies are deemed productive, valuable, and legitimate and which are marked for regulation, exclusion, or erasure. Disability is thus inseparable from the broader matrices of class, race, gender, and colonial histories that define legal embodiment, a site where law meets the corporeal to both discipline and govern.[16] The law operates not merely as a neutral arbiter but as a mechanism of biopolitical governance, crafting disability as a means of managing populations and legitimizing hierarchies of power and utility.

Under this framework, disability functions as both a juridical and biopolitical tool, a boundary marker distinguishing the included from the excluded, the normative from the deviant, and the productive from the expendable. Legal embodiment here is not passive but deeply active, rendering some bodies as sites of legal protection and visibility while exposing others to precarity, control, or abandonment. The law's ability to define not only how life is governed but which lives are deemed worthy of living at all.[17] In this context, the disabled body often becomes a site of necropolitical determination, its value contingent upon its utility to the capitalist and neoliberal order.

Historically, legal and medical discourses have coalesced to pathologize bodies deemed deviant, rendering them subject to institutionalization, sterilization, and exclusion. These practices were not isolated instances of oppression but integral to the eugenics movements of the late nineteenth and early twentieth centuries, which codified the expendability of certain populations.[18] Disability, in this sense, has operated as a legal designation that authorizes the biopolitical management of life and death, reinforcing social norms and economic imperatives. Crucially, this exclusion has always been uneven: people with similar impairments who occupied positions of social or economic power often escaped this disabling categorization, protected by their privilege and utility to dominant systems.

Americans in the late nineteenth century would have been familiar with disabled people, particularly Civil War veterans. Adrienne Phelps Coco found in a study of Chicago's 1881 ugly law, which was considerably broader than Portland's ugly law, that these laws were enforced when it came to beggars, but "disabled workers, veterans, and freak show performers whom contemporary cultural standards accepted as prominent members of public culture" were largely accepted into broader public culture.[19] Ugly laws specifically penalized *impoverished* people with disabilities; however, what made someone disabled varied significantly. Nonetheless, disabilities such as "lameness" and epilepsy are consistently recognized as specifically "unsightly." Although there are no specific records of the amount of people in Illinois' poorhouses, Cook found that in 1884: 30,130 "disabled" people resided in poorhouses in Illinois as opposed to 22,896 "able-bodied" people. 4,885 of these "disabled" people were lame or crippled, 1,648 were paralytic, 2,600 were epileptic, and 7,780 were simply "sick."[20] The enforcement of ugly laws declined over time. By the early 1900s it "simply fined people with disabilities for appearing in public."[21] These laws were largely forgotten by the mid-twentieth century, yet remained in the legal codex.

Epilepsy, the Law, and Bias

Even though ugly laws may have not been fully implemented in the 1920s, people with epilepsy were still routinely hidden from public sight by sending them to "colonies" or institutions. The most notable court case on epilepsy involving these institutions is *Buck v. Bell*. Carrie Buck was a "feeble minded woman" who was committed to a State mental institution, labeled an epileptic colony. Carrie was a poor white woman labeled as promiscuous. She became pregnant, later testifying that the nephew of the foster parents she lived with had sexually assaulted her. Her mother lived at the same epileptic colony she would come to live in as well—the Virginia Colony for Epileptics. The diagnosis of "feeble-minded" was expansive during the early 1900s. Historian Sarah F. Rose notes that institutions who accepted feeble-minded might not distinguish between a variety of diagnoses from intellectual disabilities, what would come be known as post-traumatic stress disorder, and blindness among others.[22] Carrie was the second generation of "feeble-minded people" in her family—her daughter was the third. The State of Virginia, like many other states at the time, regularly sterilized people who lived in mental institutions. Carrie fought the sterilization, arguing that it violated her Fourteenth Amendment rights. She ultimately lost to the Supreme Court. Justice Oliver Wendell Holmes Jr. wrote the major opinion of *Buck v. Bell* in 1927:

> We have seen more than once that the public welfare may call upon the best citizens for their lives. It would be strange if it could not call upon those who already sap the strength of the State for these lesser sacrifices, often not felt to be such by those concerned, in order to prevent our being swamped with incompetence. It is better for all the world if, instead of waiting to execute degenerate offspring for crime or to let them starve for their imbecility, society can prevent those who are manifestly unfit from continuing their kind... Three generations of imbeciles are enough.

Justice Holmes' decision utilizes rhetoric common to the time, such as that of Dr. John Schwartz. Schwartz was the Assistant Physician at the Ohio Hospital for Epileptics. In 1920 Schwartz opined, "a great many of these are unrestricted and allowed to propagate their species only adds to the existing misery, this is a big mistake and a gross injustice to the people of our State."[23] Holmes' argument that disabled individuals are drains upon federal welfare, and their sterilization is a sacrifice for the betterment of society directly dovetails with the language of figures such as John Schwartz. There is a chance that Holmes did not see himself as cruel, but as upholding the law according to the judicial activist approach to the Constitution, in which one interprets the Constitution in light of contemporary politics. It was already normal practice to sterilize BBIPOC, disabled, and poor women. Holmes goes on to state that this statute may even cover the removal of both fallopian tubes—a procedure I pursued.

Epileptics were considered similar to feeble-minded individuals. Paul Lombardo notes that in 1893, it was commonly believed that epilepsy would lead to "physical and moral degeneracy."[24] My own diagnosis would cause the same effects that were used to support the case to sterilize Carrie—degeneracy. Moral degeneracy was used to condemn working-class women, often those who were raising children by themselves. Scientists at the time believed that moral degeneracy was an inherited trait. The moral cost as well as financial cost of preventing the continuation of degeneracy was a social and political cause. Much of Carrie's trial reflected the prejudices of the time. Individuals who had never met Carrie, but had heard of her, created stories that contributed to the narrative of her feeble-mindedness. During that same moment, laws to limit the ability of non-disabled people and disabled people were being readily debated. These laws were interwoven with other discussions of "racial purity," which extended directly to the prevention of interracial relationships.[25]

Buck v. Bell highlighted the fact that even the social and political protections of whiteness only extended so far. If one was poor and disabled, whiteness was not a protective shield. Overwhelmingly, eugenics campaigns tended to criminalize specific bodies—disabled, female, non-white, and poor bodies were often the specific targets. White reformers used eugenics campaigns as ways to pose themselves as Other to these bodies. Nicole Rafter argues that one eugenicist, Josephine Shaw Lowell, used this rhetoric to mark herself as a "true" woman.[26] The ability to be a mother set herself apart from the "false" women who could not give birth or become pregnant. Normative bodies provide a lens by which all other bodies are to be assessed, measured, and legislated both for and against.

Martha Nussbuam notes that people with disabilities often experience both disgust and shame due to the fact that their bodies remind abled people of their own fragility.[27] She argues that frequently people with disabilities are thought of as "atypical" due to our society being organized in such a way that many people without disabilities do not regularly interact with non-abled people. People with disabilities are "unusual" and "flawed," in a way that abled people are not. Nussbaum quotes Erving Goffman discussing blind people learning to wear sunglasses so as to not upset sighted people with their eyes.[28] People with disabilities are stigmatized due to our existence, making abled people aware of their own fragility. Ultimately, we will all one day be disabled, whether that be by age or due to a late onset disability, and people with disabilities act as a reminder of this fact.

The stigmatization of people with disabilities not only allows people to direct their anxieties onto an external being, it also allows them to feel some sense of superiority. Nussbaum writes:

> Normals know that their bodies are frail and vulnerable, but when they can stigmatize the physically disabled they feel a lot better about their own human weakness. They feel really all alright, almost immortal… With the mentally disabled around them…and stigmatized as "morons," "idiots," "Mongoloid idiots," or "crazy people," normals feel positively sage and brilliant.[29]

The task of not only differentiating people with disabilities from the public, but also the systemic categorization and stigmatization functions because it comforts abled people. Certainly the argument in favor of removing people with epilepsy from the public mirrors this sentiment. According to Henderson, people with epilepsy simply cannot be allowed in public, because our seizures will traumatize others. Better to hide people with disabilities away than to think through the nature of one's anxieties surrounding the body. *Buck v. Bell* established this anxiety as good law in the United States, and it continues to be good law. This case ensured that the law continues to uphold the oppression of disabled people rather than affirming our dignity and freedom.

The Americans with Disabilities Act

The twentieth century saw a drastic shift in the perspectives of people with disabilities, such as epilepsy. After the Holocaust, the United States began to distance itself from its own eugenicist history, and its connections with Nazi eugenicists. In many ways, this culminated with the passage of the American with Disabilities Act (ADA) in 1990. The law defines disability as "a physical or mental impairment that substantially limits one or more major life activities of an individual."[30] The American with Disabilities Act (ADA) protects people with epilepsy from explicit discrimination; however, people with epilepsy may be precluded from certain spaces and experiences due to stigma. For example, if a building is not fully ADA compliant and could be a risk if someone were to seize, could dissuade someone from living there or holding employment in the facilities. Likewise, if a building has lights which intermittently flicker, a person with epilepsy may experience it as a hostile space for them. People with epilepsy may find their lives limited not due to explicit discrimination, but to the physical and social topographies of a given space. This is frequently termed the "social model" of disability, coined by Mike Oliver, which argues that it is society which determines whether a condition is disabling or not.[31] People experience variations of impairment due to the spaces which they frequent. The law, as a discourse formulated by people, may further these social impairments.

Within the United States, people with epilepsy may drive within every State. However, there is a prohibition of time from driving after having had a seizure, such as 90 days. In these states, it is frequently up to the person or their physician to report their seizure. For example, as of 2024, Maryland requires an individual be seizure-free for 90 days and have an individual risk assessment by a Medical Advisory Board; however, "[t]reating physicians recommended driving for 84.4% of applications rejected by the MAB."[32] The regulation of people with epilepsy's ability to drive is haphazard at best due to the importance of self-reportage. People who never or rarely experience tonic clonic seizures but only a myoclonic jerk could be subject to the same penalties as someone with treatment resistant seizures. There is a significant level of bias toward people with epilepsy and perceived experiences of stigma. Moreover, those experiences increase over time, "[t]hose patients who had 6–10 years duration of illness were more than four times...more likely to develop perceived stigma than those patients who had one year duration of illness...."[33] A study in 2013 reported that people without epilepsy frequently experienced anxiety around developing close relationships with people with epilepsy.[34] The study goes on to demonstrate that people without epilepsy are not biased toward people with epilepsy in the abstract sense; however, when it comes to concrete relationships, they report active avoidance. A study found that people with epilepsy experience "depression at two to three times the rate of the general population and are more likely to suffer from depression than people with other chronic conditions. Approximately one in five of all adults who experience epilepsy suffer generalized anxiety disorder...."[35] People with epilepsy who experience stigma report high levels of depression and decreased quality of life due to their depression.[36] Although epilepsy is a very common neurological condition, people with epilepsy still report experiences of stigma and prejudice which limit their abilities to gain employment or build fulfilling relationships.[37]

Although people with epilepsy are protected by law, they are not protected from the socially disabling effects of their condition. The law articulates protections such as walking, hearing, seeing, and speaking as major life activities. It overlooks the expansion of technological assists which have contributed to people with disabilities' participation and inclusion in public life. The ADA serves as a vehicle to make clear what facets of life a person with a disability can *legally* experience. It also enforces a specific vision of what it means to be disabled or not, which often occludes sociopolitical topographies. Ron Amundson critiques the ADA, noting these activities are not necessary for life, and it disregards the technology that allows people to live and thrive "with impairments."[38] Moreover, the

ADA fails to account for the ways in which people with disabilities' lives are actively constricted through bias, stigma, and prejudice.

I have often worked and lived in places which were not-ADA compliant. Yet, it was never made clear to me how to pursue a claim. Moreover, I never knew whether the process would involve time or money, both of which I lacked. As a result, the idea of forcing ADA compliance, even though I ought to have accessible housing and workplaces since it is my right, is something that even now I balk at. I do not assert my rights because I have never felt as though it was possible for me to do so. If I don't dare to assert my rights, do I have them? Or will I struggle to live and work in places unsafe for me.

I have a rare form of epilepsy that does not respond to traditional treatment and requires surgical interventions such as the Vagus Nerve Stimulation (VNS) implant, which I have, along with medication.[39] It is unclear to the extent to which the ADA protects me, when I am not seizing. The strength of the ADA itself, as a vehicle for equal protection, is also unclear. In 1997, Patricia Garrett and Milton Ash sued the Alabama government using the ADA. They argued Alabama had not done enough for their disabilities. Garret was demoted from her position at the University of Alabama of Birmingham after she took a leave from work for radiation and chemotherapy treatments. Ash had asthma and was denied a request to modify his work duties so as to reduce his exposure to cigarette smoke and carbon monoxide. Their case could only work if the ADA could be enforced through the Fourteenth Amendment. Chief Justice William Rehnquist found that the ADA does not apply, "so long as their actions towards such individuals are rational States are not required by the Fourteenth Amendment to make special accommodations for the disabled. They could quite hard headedly–and perhaps hardheartedly–hold to job-qualification requirements which do not make allowance for the disabled."[40] Discrimination against people with disabilities through a refusal to accommodate our needs is rational, and as Jamal Greene notes, this ruling undermined Congressional ability to enforce accommodation by the states. This state-by-state approach actively undermines the rights of people with disabilities, and further troubles questions of accessibility.[41]

It is difficult to obtain accommodations *if* they are available, and the act of asking for one's dignity to be recognized is a fraught experience. Often, when I disclose a certain displeasure with the idea of asking for accommodation, it is due in fact to my class background. I never felt empowered to demand aid. I asked for accommodations in college timidly, afraid to use them, knowing I would not do well without using them, and yet fearful just the same. To exercise one's rights, to demand them, is to feel a sense of empowerment and ability to do so. However, as in my situation, it is a distinct possibility that vulnerable people may not feel comfortable doing so and may lack support systems who can assist them. Yet, there is a possibility that behind my own experience is a sensation of shame, emerging due to ableism and stigma.

Shame and Access

Shame is a social emotion; Jóhannsdóttir, Probyn, and Lehtinen (1998) all find that individuals who have been shamed have a greater capacity to re-experience shame.[42] Individuals with disabilities often "conceal" their disabilities from others, and this is particularly easy for people such as myself, whose disabilities are liminally visible. Unless I were to seize or a person saw my medical alert tattoo, it would be shocking for them to identify me with epilepsy. Goffman; Dayapoglu, Ayyıldız, and Şeker find that people with epilepsy in particular feel a decrease in fear of stigma if they do not disclose their disability.[43] Shame is bound up with other social positions such as race, gender, nationality, and class among other such positionalities. Identities intersect with one another, shaping one's experiences of shame or lack thereof.

Shame is an emotion which Nussbuam points to as creating a narrative of otherness. It can separate a person from the greater whole. People with epilepsy often experience significant shame and find themselves feeling very disabled due to stigma and fears surrounding how others would respond to their disclosure.

I am unsure if the discomfort I feel in asserting my rights is due to shame. However, in moments of disclosure I rapidly witness a change in a person's perspective of myself. I move from a person who is independent to someone whose body is unpredictable, and I may become deeply vulnerable. In that moment, the other person would be responsible for me. The shift highlights at once fears of people with disabilities and bodies that may betray us, which occasionally turns into a fear for me, in which the other person asks a litany of questions about accessibility. It is easier to not disclose, and to hope I do not seize. I try not to think of my epilepsy, even though it is a constant companion. I will never be seizure-free, and I will never be unable to think of the world in terms of threats.

Self-disclosure pushes me into a space of hyper-visibility, something I have always hidden from. My discomfort, and often refusal to self-disclose, is no doubt informed by ableism. *During my early 20s, I received Social Security Disability Insurance (SSDI). I had to prove my disability and its deleterious impact on my life. I had to chronicle what at the time I found to be embarrassing accounts of seizures, the inevitable blood, wounds, and possible urine or defecation afterwards. My inability to think during school due to brain fog, or my capability to hold a cohesive experience of the day due to absence seizures led to me performing poorly. I also needed to prove my financial need. The process, at the time, felt too revealing, too shameful. Yet, I knew I was lucky. Many individuals apply to SSDI numerous times and are unable to receive the benefits.*

The repeated denial of SSDI demonstrates necropolitics—the power to decide who lives and who dies—by using bureaucratic systems that make certain lives unlivable. The State forces individuals to navigate a punitive and exclusionary process that systematically denies many of the resources needed to sustain their existence. Those deemed unworthy of support are denied life-sustaining benefits, pushing them to the margins of survival. This reinforces the idea that only bodies capable of productivity within a capitalist framework are deserving of recognition and support.[44] The denial of SSDI benefits, therefore, is not merely an administrative decision; it exemplifies the State's power to enforce precarity and death through bureaucratic indifference.

The rigid evidentiary and legal standards that SSDI applicants must meet also reflect the ways queer individuals are often required to conform to heteronormative legal frameworks to access rights or recognition.[45] The SSDI system polices bodies and identities, prioritizing those that fit a State-sanctioned narrative of suffering and compliance while excluding those who cannot or will not conform. This policing enacts a form of legal embodiment, rendering disabled bodies hyper-visible and subject to intense scrutiny while erasing their lived experiences in favor of bureaucratic and medicalized narratives. By combining necropolitics and queer legal theory, we see that the SSDI process is more than a site of denial—it is a mechanism for enforcing societal norms that devalue, and control bodies deemed unproductive, deviant, or expendable.[46]

However, my experience required me to lay bare the most intimate moments of my life in which I had been the most vulnerable and asked for those moments to be dire enough to need aid. Afterward, I avoided disclosing my disability, even though my seizures were frequent enough to necessitate significant limits on my life, many of which I violated to experience what would it be like to live *without* fear or shame.

Shame and hyper-visibility are unable to be extricated from one another, particularly within a legal landscape in which to receive governmental assistance, one must plead that one is too disabled to live without it. To access social services is a vulnerable process as well as a legal process. One's body and life become hyper-visible; a spotlight is placed upon one's disability and struggles in life due to this disability.

My memories and experiences of my early 20s are inseparable from the process of obtaining SSDI. I cried when I received it, knowing that I could see my specialists and try numerous medications, and perhaps discover why my epilepsy would not respond to medication. It provided me with a diagnosis, and a medical implant which for the most part controls my seizures. Occasionally they break through, bringing me to a halt, but largely the exist in the background. Despite these significant positives, the requirements to receive SSDI and the accompanying emotional and psychological tolls contributed to me feeling more disabled than before I had SSDI.

SSDI contributed to a heightened awareness of the disabling impacts of my then nameless form of epilepsy, and the resultant depression and anxiety further disabled me, contributing to fears and anxieties around disclosure.[47] Now, those fears are minimized, but I frequently decide to not disclose my disability so as to avoid the deleterious emotional and psychological effects of visibility.

Meaningfulness or Meaninglessness: The Problem of Disability

Within the liberal conception of the State, people with disabilities are not able to be considered full political actors. The political actor within liberalism is autonomous, rational, and pursues their own interests. This is not a reality for many people with disabilities, including myself. I can never live alone, and when I seize I am rendered incapable of thinking rationally for hours at a time. According to the liberal conceptions of the State and society, my life then, lacks full meaningfulness. Hans S. Reinders outlines the problems of liberalism for people with disabilities as bound up with questions of a meaningful life:

> The prevalent idea in contemporary culture that creating meaning is an individual activity has serious implications for human beings to whom the notion of agency does not apply. It is this very ideal that makes their lives appear to be deficient. Where there is no agent, there must be a deficit of meaning. Where there is a deficit of meaning, it is difficult not to perceive human existence as the cause of grave suffering. If it is merely a cause of great suffering, the question of why these people are kept alive becomes hard to avoid indeed. Not only is it hard to avoid, but it also appears to have a definite answer. The centrality of agency and all that it stands for-'choice', 'decision', 'freedom', 'self-determination', and so on-is the default position of liberal culture. It makes us blind to other dimensions of our existence, such as our lack of control, our vulnerability, and our dependence on other people. For this very reason, it also makes accepting disabled people as human beings in their own right, without expecting them to meet contemporary standards of success, a difficult task indeed. Within liberal culture, the question of whether profoundly disabled lives have meaning in themselves creates a vexing, almost paralyzing problem.[48]

Is a life more or less meaningful if one can never access liberal perspectives of a "good life"? By virtue of being locked out of liberal personhood, people with disabilities can become seen as "nonpersons" due to inability to fully participate in public life. John Rawls argues that moral persons are defined by their capacity to have a conception of the good and have a sense of justice. This inherently locks out people with significant mental disabilities who may not be able to participate. What then is the status of nonpersons? For Rawls, and including other liberals such as Englehardt, liberal public morality must rely on moral sources that cannot be necessarily included in public morality, such as religious compunctions.

Englehardt utilizes a consequentialist framework when broaching people with disabilities' rights and place in society. He argues outright that people with disabilities may ultimately be human nonpersons, "Not all humans are self-conscious, rational, and able to conceive of the possibility of blaming and praising. Fetuses, infants, the profoundly mentally retarded, and the hopelessly comatose provide examples of human nonpersons. They are members of the human species but do not in and of themselves have standing in the secular moral community."[49] Obligations to nonpersons arises from theories of usefulness because the, "sense of person cannot be justified in terms of the basic grammar of morality (i.e. because such entities do not have intrinsic moral standing through being moral agents), one will need rather to justify a social sense of person in terms of the usefulness of the practice of treatment certain entities as if they were persons."[50] The value of people with disabilities is justified by reference to other persons, rather than by their intrinsic worth as human beings. Liberalism's requirement that we detach ourselves and examine our lives with a level of objective rationality precludes the fact that as persons, we have a worth outside of our usefulness to the social order. We find that worth in external moral principles, that according to liberalism *cannot* be a part of public morality because they may require constraints upon our rights. This perspective operates broadly within the law.

The theory of legal expressiveness argues that the law demonstrates the State's perspective and priorities.[51] This ideology is not confined to history books—it persists today, embedded in systems like SSDI. Likewise, through the process of SSDI, people with disabilities are expected to disclose significant, sometimes painful information that other individuals are not required to do in countries with robust welfare provisions. In the United States, however, the process reflects an underlying ableism inherent to liberal conceptions of personhood, which equate value with independence, productivity, and self-sufficiency.[52] By these standards, disabled people are systematically positioned as "less than" their able-bodied peers, forced into hyper-visibility to access even basic support.

Our legislation reflects the ableism inherent to liberal conceptions of personhood. We are less than our able-bodied peers. This visibility—the necessity to constantly prove one's worth under the watchful eye of a system steeped in ableist ideology—is not an act of empowerment but a stark reminder of exclusion. The law's priorities are clear: it values those who can assimilate into capitalist frameworks of productivity over those who cannot. The SSDI process is just one of many examples where the legal framework functions as both a mirror of societal bias and a tool for perpetuating inequality.

These legal frameworks for understanding disability lack a comprehensive and intersectional analysis to address inequality and mitigate the harm of ableism. Although the ADA has eradicated blatantly ableist laws such as ugly laws, people with disabilities are disproportionately impacted by legislation which specifically targets impoverished people. The 2024 amici curiae brought to the Supreme Court of the United States in the case *City of Grants Pass, Oregon v. Gloria Johnson*, et al., *on Behalf of Themselves and All Others Similarly Situated*, describes the contemporary impacts of Oregon's anti-homelessness law. They argue ordinances against homelessness passed in Grants Pass, Oregon uniquely impact people with disabilities:

> Less than 5% of housing in the United States is accessible for moderate mobility disabilities, and less than 1% is accessible for wheelchair use. Housing costs are prohibitive for many disabled people who rely on public assistance for basic costs of living— the average cost of a one-bedroom apartment in the United States exceeds the maximum monthly Supplemental Security Income a person can receive.[53]

It is largely known within the disabled community that SSDI is not enough to independently live on. In the early 2010s I received a little over $700 a month, and with the restrictions on how much income I could make a month, made it impossible to live independently. People with disabilities routinely live in a normalized state of precarity, and "[h]omeless people are significantly more likely to have disabilities compared to both the United States population at large and individuals living in poverty."[54] The 2023 annual report by the US Department of Housing and Urban Development (HUD) recorded that one in every three individuals experiencing chronic homelessness have a disability.[55] The majority of housing in the United States is inaccessible to people with mobility disabilities, and in a shortage of housing, people with disabilities are faced with the possibility of homelessness at a greater rate than people without disabilities.

Homeless shelters, particularly short-term homeless shelters, are not always guaranteed to be accessible. Disability Law United and Newman McNulty filed a lawsuit in 2025 against temporary homeless shelters in Denver Colorado that violated the ADA. In a letter written to Denver City Council members, the City Attorney's Office, and Mayor Mike Johnston they detail multiple examples of discrimination:

> Christopher Haworth, a man with cerebral palsy who uses a wheelchair, says he was denied entry at Denver Rescue Mission shelters when they didn't have accessible beds available.
> He was kicked out, on other occasions, because of the size of his wheelchair.
> He was also denied admission by the Denver Rescue Mission's Lawrence Street Shelter because staff considered his epilepsy a liability.
> Mindy Polson, who uses a colostomy bag, told Denverite the staff at the 48th Street Women's Shelter denied her the sharp medical scissors she

> needed to cut open her bag, so she was left trying to use nail clippers instead.
> She damaged her colon in the process, which led to an infection. When she complained to shelter staff they continued to refuse to allow her access to medical scissors. She damaged her colon more and was eventually asked to leave the shelter. She claims she was kicked out in retaliation.[56]

McNulty's stated goal is to compel the city and city-funded shelters to comply with the ADA. The letter was sent in late 2024, and with winter, McNulty expressed concerns over Denver's inaction. Homeless shelters are not in and of themselves guaranteed to be safe and accessible places, and this places homeless people with disabilities in dangerous situations.

Anti-homelessness legislation rarely is accompanied by corresponding legislation to aid people with homelessness, much less assist homeless people with disabilities. Much like ugly laws, these forms of legislation act as a way to "clear" the streets from "unsightly" people, which frequently includes people with disabilities. Laws which criminalize homelessness consistently negatively impact people with disabilities; nonetheless, people with disabilities are frequently overlooked. Unlike ugly laws which highlighted poor people with disabilities, contemporary anti-homeless legislation attempts to make poor people with disabilities invisible.

When we use the eye of the State, people with disabilities are made both hyper-visible and invisible. Hyper-visibility has been a tool for people with disabilities to make significant advances; however, that same visibility may be traumatizing. Invisibility allows the State to develop and pass legislation which will disproportionately impact people with disabilities while not breaking anti-discrimination laws. One pathway forward is to use Rachel Adams' model of "choosing disability," in which legislation but also society must be pressured to foreground people with disabilities in a meaningful way, to do so requires a theoretical shift—one away from liberal conceptions of personhood and autonomy, to one of interdependence.[57] Part of choosing disability is to move away from a dichotomy in which I am disabled and you are not. It means embracing the vulnerability that is essential to our existence, and to consider ourselves as part of a community rather than as atomised into distinct categories based on our current capacities.

Eli Clare writes about stolen bodies, "There are so many ways oppression and social injustice can mark a body, steal a body, feed lies and poison to a body."[58] Stereotypes and the "false images" of what a body *ought* to look like may haunt a body "stealing it away as surely as bullets."[59]

My body is shaped by my disability. My voice wavers, and my throat which subconsciously clenches in pain, as the electricity shoots into my brain. The pain that follows me from injuries sustained while seizing. The invisible ghosts of fear and shame that haunt me, shaping my daily decisions and indecisions.

According to Clare, part of reconfiguring the world, reshaping the material conditions that directly impact people with disabilities necessitates changes in what we believe about our bodies, and what we believe about others' bodies. This requires a turning toward our vulnerability, toward the material realities of disability that disability law may occlude. The language of the law sanitizes the reality of disability, and in the process, it has the capacity to estrange us from our bodies.

The ease of my body changes, depending on my health. After two recent significant tonic clonic seizures, I needed time to return to myself. My body ached, and felt distinctly separate from myself. Like many people with epilepsy, I often differentiate my brain from my mind.[60] *My brain is the organ that I cannot control. My mind is my home, but after seizures I am estranged from my mind. It is foggy, difficult to return to. I am unmoored. I am no longer myself, but in Clare's conception I am always myself. My brain and my mind are not dichotomous beings. Both are essential to my experience of the world and of being.*

This turn toward our bodies is how we choose disability, when we choose disability, we open up other possibilities of choosing vulnerabilities.

The seizing of my disability and all disabilities shifts the visibility of disability from the eye of the State and the law to that of people with disabilities.*The factical part of having epilepsy is that my body is, at times, uncontrollable, an entity foreign to me. I know only the before and after of my seizures, but in choosing to prioritize disability I have to reconsider what is considered a normative part of life. This full acceptance includes embracing the realities of seizures, with lost time, bodily waste, and pain.*

My body is ultimately vulnerable, and a disability first framework of law must be based on vulnerability. Our bodies are at all times possibly in need of others for care. A conception of the law that focuses solely upon the rational autonomous actor misses the reality of being, which is vulnerability.[61]

If we choose disability in the law and in society, we can dismantle the power of disgust and shame in the law. These two emotional motivators have guided the law as it pertains to disability but also appear in other forms of the law that seek to regulate our bodies, namely in sexuality and gender. Disgust manifests itself in distancing ourselves from that which we find repellant. In contrast, shame causes hiding. In both cases, people and the State project onto marginalized groups their anxieties and fears which they want to conceal. Nussbaum argues that insecurities around sexuality, gender, and ability lead to people constituting themselves as "normals" and asking sexual minorities and minorities in terms of physical and mental ability to conceal themselves.[62] The hiding away of people with disabilities and LGBTQ+ people from our public forums contributes to reifying ideologies of power in which we continue to be nonpersons within liberal conception of personhood. Moreover, it upholds liberal individualism which distances us from one another. However, we can never be and will never be free from one another and our mutual obligations for one another. Rather than avoid these obligations, we ought to attend to them carefully and recognize that these obligations contribute to a broader political ethic of care.

Responsibility for Others: Reconfiguring Care and the Law

Reinders offers the following claim in defense of our responsibility for others:

> To accept responsibility for other people, we must regard our own lives in terms of those relationships. That is to say, only when we regard our own lives as received from others that have accepted responsibility for us. will we be able to assist and support those who have nothing to offer in terms of reciprocating our actions. Even if it is often suggested that it is 'rational' to act on the principle *do ut des*, the constitution of human life is such that this principle is more appropriately reversed: we can give because -- and to the extent that -- we have been and continuously are given…The demand that we care for other person's life is rooted in the fact of our indebtedness for all the things we have received: intelligence, meanings, speech, love, and much more.[63]

Reinders' argument is in accord with the major principles of care ethics. The undergirding assumption of care ethics is that we have mutual and shared obligations, and that our morality is shaped by our fulfilling these obligations. Care ethics is a contextual ethic, it aligns closely with Aristotlean virtue ethics, in which those obligations are bound up with who that person is. For example, a person who cannot provide care due to significant mental impairment will not have the same expectations as a fully abled person who comes from significant socioeconomic privileges. The strength of care ethics, particularly in the scope of disability, is that it focuses upon our relations with one another, both direct relations and more indirect ones that we experience through taxation, for example.

Care ethics necessitates a reframing of our beliefs of *who* is able to have a meaningful life, and this ability must be based on something other than reason, autonomy, and other characteristics necessary for liberalism. Rather, it must be based on the fact that human beings' worth is not derived from others but must be found elsewhere. People with disabilities matter due to the fact that they are persons. Much research demonstrates that children with significant disabilities are meaningful and important to their families.[64] Similarly, communities such as the L'Arche Houses express mutuality with persons with disabilities through living in community *with* people with disabilities. As we turn toward the role of disgust and shame in "Don't Say Gay" laws, we ought to consider how choosing disability can prepare the way for a broader political and legal framework.

NOTES

1. Rosemarie Garland-Thomson, "Misfits: A Feminist Materialist Disability Concept," *Hypatia* 26. No.3(2011).
2. Thomas D. Russell, "BUCK v. BELL, Superintendent of State Colony Epileptics and Feeble Minded, 274 US 200 (1927)," *American Legal History-Russell*, 18; Adam Cohen, *Imbeciles: The Supreme Court, American Eugenics, and the Sterilization of Carrie Buck* (Penguin Books, 2017).
3. Michel Foucault, *Discipline and Punish.*
4. Nancy J. Hirschmann, "Disability as a New Frontier for Feminist Intersectionality Research," *Politics & Gender* 8, no.3(2012): 401.
5. "Disability Characteristics," *Census,* https://data.census.gov/table?q=disability.

6. Carol Gilligan, *In a Different Voice: Moral Psychology and Women's Development* (Cambridge: Harvard University Press, 1982).
7. Riley Clare Valentine cannot and will never be able to drive due to their particular form of epilepsy.
8. Simon J. Williams, "Bodily Dys-order: Desire, Excess and the Transgression of Corporeal Boundaries," *Body & Society* 4, no.2(1998): 59–82.
9. Susan Schweik, *The Ugly Laws: Disability in Public* (New York: New York University Press, 2009), 89.
10. Susan Schweik, "Kicked to the Curb: Ugly Law Then and Now," *HARV. CR-CLL REV.* 46 (2011): 2.
11. Ibid.
12. Susan Schweik, *The Ugly Laws,* 89.
13. Ibid.
14. Douglas C. Baynton, "Disability and the Justification of Inequality in American History," *The Disability Studies Reader* 17, no.33(2013): 42.
15. Ibid., 39.
16. Michel Foucault, *Discipline and Punish*; Michel Foucault, *The History of Sexuality Volume I* (New York: Pantheon Books, 1978).
17. Achille Mbembe, "Necropolitics," *Public Culture* 15, no. 1 (2003): 11–40.
18. Rosemarie Garland-Thomson, "Theorizing Disability," *Extraordinary Bodies: Figuring Physical Disability in American Culture and Literature* (1997): 19–54.
19. Adrienne Phelps Coco, "Diseased, Maimed, Mutilated: Categorizations of Disability and an Ugly Law in Late Nineteenth-Century Chicago," *Journal of Social History* 44, no.1(2010): 25.
20. Ibid., 34.
21. Ibid.
22. Sarah F. Rose, *No Right to Be Idle* (UNC Press, 2017), 25.
23. John Schwartz, "Heredity as a Factor in Epilepsy," *The Ohio State Institution Journal* 2, no.3(1920): 53–54; Djem Kissiov, Taylor Dewall, and Bruce Hermann, "The Ohio Hospital for Epileptics – The First 'Epilepsy Colony' in America," *Epilepsia* 54, no.4(2013): 1524–1534.
24. Paul A. Lombardo, *Three Generations, No Imbeciles: Eugenics, The Supreme Court, and* Buck v. Bell (Baltimore: Johns Hopkins University Press, 2022), 13.

25. Ibid., 45.
26. Nicole H. Rafter, "Claims-Making and Socio-Cultural Context in the First U.S. Eugenics Campaign," *Social Problems* 39, no.1(1992): 26.
27. Martha Nussbaum, *Hiding from Humanity,* 296.
28. Ibid., 293.
29. Ibid., 219.
30. "American with Disabilities Act," 42(2008).
31. Mike Oliver, "The Social Model of Disability: Thirty Years On," *Disability & Society* 28, no.7(2013).
32. Brandy B. Ma, et al. "Regulating Drivers with Epilepsy in Maryland: Results of the Application of a United States Consensus Guideline," *Epilepsia* 58,no.8(2017): 4.
33. Najma Iqbal Malik, et al., "Perceived Stigma, Discrimination and Psychological Problems Among Patients with Epilepsy," *Front Psychiatry* (2022).
34. W. Cui, R. Kobau, M. M. Zack, J. M. Buelow, and K. A. Joan, "Recent Changes in Attitudes of US Adults toward People with Epilepsy - Results from the 2005 Summer Styles and 2013 Fall Styles Surveys," *Epilepsy & Behavior* 52(2015): 108–118.
35. Malik, et al. "Perceived Stigma."
36. Zerrin Yildirim, "Stigma Accounts for Depression in Patients with Epilepsy," *Epilepsy Behav* (2018); Janhavi Ajit Vaingankar, "Understanding the Relationships Between Mental Disorders, Self-reported Health Outcomes and Positive Mental Health: Findings from a National Survey," *Health Qual Life Outcomes* (2020); Jéssica Lopes de Souza, et al. "The Perceived Social Stigma of People with Epilepsy with Regard to the Question of Employability," *Neurol Res Int*(2018).
37. de Souza, "The Perceived Social Stigma."
38. Ron Amundson, "Disability, Ideology, and Quality of Life: A Bias in Biomedical Ethics," in *Genetic Testing, Healthcare, and Disability,* eds. David Wasserman, Jerome Bickerbach, and Robert Wachbrot (Cambridge University Press, 2005), 122.
39. Ali A. Asadi-Pooya, Mehdi Bazrafshan, and Mohen Farazdaghi, "Cluster Analysis of a Large Dataset of Patients with Lennox-Gastaut Syndrome," *Seizure* 92(2021): 36–39; Stéphane Auvin et al., "The Impact of Seizure Frequency on Quality of Life in Patients with Lennox-Gastaut Syndrome or Dravet Syndrome,"

Epilepsy & Behavior 123(2021): 108,239; Indar Kumar Sharawat, et al., "Efficacy and Safety of Corpus Callosotomy and Ketogenic Diet in Children with Lennox-Gastaut Syndrome: A Systematic Review and Meta-analysis," *Child's Nervous* System (2021): 1–10.

40. Bd. of Trs. v. Garrett, 531 U.S. 356, 367.
41. Greene, *How Rights Went Wrong*, 185–186.
42. Ásta Jóhannsdóttir, S.T. Egilson, and K. Runswick-Cole, "Feeling Disability: Theories of Affect and Critical Disability Studies," *Disability & Society* 33, no2(2018): 197–217; Elspeth Probyn, *Blush: Faces of Shame* (Minneapolis: University of Minnesota Press, 2005); Ullaliina Lehtinen, "How Does One Know What Shame is? Epistemology, Emotions, and Forms of Life in Juxtaposition." *Hypatia* 13, no.1(1998): 56–77.
43. Erving Goffman, "Stigma and Social Identity," In *Deviance & Liberty* (Routledge, 2018), 24–31; Nuray Dayapoglu, Neşe İşcan Ayyıldız, Demet Şeker, "Fear of Negative Evaluation and the Concealment of Their Disease by Epilepsy Patients," *Epilepsy & Behavior* 113(2020).
44. Achille Mbembe, "Necropolitcs," *Public Culture* 15, no.1(2003): 11–40.
45. Judith Butler, *Undoing Gender* (New York: Routledge, 2004).
46. Jasbir K. Puar, *The Right to Maim: Debility, Capacity, Disability* (Durham: Duke University Press, 2017).
47. Riley Clare Valentine, "Willful Brains and Absent Minds: A Phenomenological Investigaiton of Fear, Epilepsy, and Willful Being," *Disability & Society.*
48. Hans S. Reinders, *The Future of the Disabled in a Liberal Society*, 205.
49. H. Tristam Jr. Englehardt, *The Foundations of Bioethics*, 2nd. edition (New York: Oxford University Press), 138–19.
50. Ibid., 147.
51. Paul A. Lombardo, *Three Generations.*
52. Eva Feder Kittay, "Anita Silvers, David Wasserman, and Mary B. Mahowald. Disability, Difference, and Discrimination: Perspectives on Justice in Bioethics and Public Policy. New York, Rowman & Littlefield, 1998," *Hypatia* 17, no. 1 (2002): 209–213.
53. *City of Grants Pass v. Johnson*, 219 L. Ed. 2d 941, 974.
54. Ibid.

55. Tanya de Sousa, et al., "The 2023 Annual Homelessness Assessment Report (AHAR) to Congress," *The U.S. Department of Housing and Urban Development*, December 2023, https://www.huduser.gov/portal/sites/default/files/pdf/2023-ahar-part-1.Pdf.
56. Kyle Harris, "Denver Contracts with Homeless Shelters that Discriminate Against Disabled People, Advocates Say," *Denverite*, December 27, 2024, https://denverite.com/2024/12/27/denver-shelters-disability-discrimination-lawsuit/.
57. Rachel Adams, "Choosing Disability, Visualizing Care," *Kennedy Institute of Ethics Journal* 27, no.2(2017): 301–321.
58. Eli Clare, "Stolen Bodies, Reclaimed Bodies: Disability and Queerness," *Public Culture* 13, no.3(2001): 363.
59. Ibid.
60. Sara Ryan and Ulla Räisänen,"'The Brain is Such a Delicate Thing': An Exploration of Fear and Seizures Among Young People with Epilepsy," *Chronic Illness* 8, no.3(2012): 214–224.
61. Riley Clare Valentine, "Willful Brains and Absent Minds."
62. Nussbaum, *Hiding from Humanity*, 296.
63. Reinders, *The Future of the Disabled*, 17.
64. Eva Feder Kittay, "The Personal is Philosophical is Political: A Philosopher and Mother of a Cognitively Disabled Person Sends Notes from the Battlefield," *Metaphilosophy* 40, no. 3-4 (2009): 606–627; Eva Feder Kittay, *Learning from My Daughter: The Value and Care of Disabled Minds* (Oxford University Press: 2019).

CHAPTER 3

Discipline and Disgust: Book Bans and "Don't Say Gay" Laws

Abstract Public education in the United States has become an increasingly salient realm of contesting political and legislative perspectives. Florida Governor Ron DeSantis' "Don't Say Gay" Bill initiated a series of nationwide anti-LGBTQ+ legislation. The bill, which is a regurgitation of past "No Promo Homo," outlaws any discussions of gender or sexuality with students. Parents may file complaints if they suspect the law is in violation, creating a surveillance apparatus in which they may act as extensions of State authority. As a result, educators have found their ability to support and care for students to be limited so as to avoid felony charges of violating the bill. Educators who are LGBTQ+ have also found themselves silenced. Transgender educators have been penalized for using titles and pronouns that reflect their gender identity. These laws mobilize disgust as a tool of power, invoking moral panic to justify the exclusion of LGBTQ+ voices from public spaces. Although LGBTQ+ people are a protected class under Title IX, these acts hope to push LGBTQ+ people out of public spaces like education and are right-wing attacks on expressions of gender and sexuality which do not align with right-wing cisheterosexual patriarchal Judeo-Christian values.

Keywords Public education · Disgust · "Don't Say Gay," "No Promo Homo," exclusion

R. C. Valentine and Z. McNeill, *The Coercive Power of the Law*,
https://doi.org/10.1007/978-3-032-07589-5_3

Schools have become a central battleground in the fight over queer and trans rights.[1] With limited legal protections, queer and transgender youth remain among the most vulnerable to regulation, surveillance, and erasure—especially within educational institutions.[2] At the State level, legislative attacks increasingly target both bodies and the knowledge, history, and identities they carry—because erasing history and controlling knowledge is also a way of disciplining the body itself.[3]

As noted in the Supreme Court case *Bethel School District v. Fraser*, public schools are tasked with "inculcat[ing]the habits and manners of civility" and teaching students "the boundaries of socially appropriate behavior."[4] This means that schools often enforce societal norms and constructed boundaries of identity through discipline and surveillance. Schools do not merely transmit knowledge; they produce subjects. As Foucault writes, discipline "produces subjected and practiced bodies, 'docile' bodies"—and in the contemporary context, these bodies are shaped by implicit assumptions about sexuality, gender, and propriety. The child becomes both a product and target of State-sanctioned heteronormativity.[5]

By omitting or censoring queer histories, lifestyles, and teachings, schools purposefully convey to children that queerness is undesirable or contaminating.[6] Through these teachings—and the discipline that follows when they are disrupted—children learn "which bodies come to matter –and why."[7] As Eve Sedgwick argues, the regulation of knowledge—what is allowed to be known, spoken, or even suspected—plays a central role in how queer subjectivities are policed and repressed.[8] Legal recognition, or its deliberate denial, becomes a key mechanism in determining which forms of sexuality are rendered visible and legitimate.[9] In this way, the law constructs sexuality not simply by prohibiting certain acts, but by shaping the very conditions under which identities can be named, claimed, and protected.[10]

As of March 2025, 25 states have enacted laws barring transgender students from participating in sports aligned with their gender identity,[11] and at least 20 states restrict access to restrooms and facilities that correspond with students' gender identities—some even criminalizing such use.[12] These laws enforce normative gender boundaries through surveillance and punishment, turning bodily movement into a site of regulation and compliance.[13] In at least 14 states, school personnel are legally required to notify a student's parents of their transgender identity before using their chosen name or pronouns.[14] This practice of forced outing and pervasive misgendering not only violates students' privacy and bodily autonomy—it actively exposes them to the possibility of harm in abusive or unsupportive home environments. As Philip Seaver-Hall explains, this forced disclosure and misgendering can "constitute harassment" and is a denial of the student's capacity to self-identify and inhabit their own body and name on their own terms.[15]

These laws and policies don't just dictate what can be said—they control how bodies are allowed to be visible, move, and be legally recognized within public spaces and institutions. Mia Fischer warns that visibility can be a trap—far from a guarantee of safety or inclusion, it often reinforces systems of control.[16] This is not a new phenomenon. As Margot Canaday points out, the heightened visibility of gay and lesbian communities during and after World War II led to a wave of intense State repression against gender and sexual nonconformity.[17]

Contemporary laws enforce a narrow definition of embodiment—legalizing misgendering, excluding non-normative sexualities, and punishing any form of deviation. This framework inflicts deep psychic, emotional, and physical harm on queer and trans youth.[18] These are not abstract legal or theoretical consequences—they are matters of life and death.

These legislative efforts are part of a broader national project to systematically erase queer and trans existence from public education.[19] Florida's 2022 "Don't Say Gay" law exemplifies this project: it restricts discussion of sexual orientation and gender identity, legally describes sex as immutable, and prohibits teachers from using a student's affirmed name or pronouns—permitting others to misgender students without repercussion.[20] Expanded in 2023 to cover all grade levels, the law codifies queer and trans erasure across the K–12 system.[21]

By 2025, 21 states had enacted similar "Don't Say Gay" laws that either restrict or require parental notification before discussing LGBTQ+ content.[22] Not only do these restrictions, as Hunter Foist argues, "chill speech" in ways that undermine both public health outcomes and First Amendment protections, but they also determine which identities are seen as valid and which are treated as deviant, dangerous, and disposable.[23]

There have also been federal efforts to implement a nationwide "Don't Say Gay" policy.[24] While legislation stalled in Congress, on January 29, 2025, President Trump signed the executive order Ending Radical Indoctrination in K–12 Schooling, banning materials deemed "anti-American" or "subversive"—including those supporting "gender ideology" or critical race theory.[25] This move, as legal scholar Robin Maril notes, is part of a broader conservative strategy to rewrite constitutional liberties by attacking substantive due process rights, including those recognized in *Lawrence v. Texas* and *Obergefell v. Hodges*.[26]

Disgust and discipline converge most visibly in the recent wave of book bans targeting queer literature. We view disgust not as an innate response, but a socially constructed affect tied to fantasies of purity and contamination. Disgust has long been used to justify the regulation of marginalized bodies, marking them as threats to the normative social order. For example, when signing the State's "Don't Say Gay" law, then-governor Ron DeSantis said that "We've seen libraries that have clearly inappropriate pornographic materials for very young kids."[27] School districts across the State pulled hundreds of books off library shelves.[28]

These acts of erasure simultaneously render queerness itself highly visible. The State bans governments, while also outing students through legislating which bathrooms they can and cannot use, alongside determining whether they can or cannot participate in sports. Queerness, much like in our analysis of disability, is a category in which visibility is frequently a weapon, used to articulate disgust and queerphobic sentiment in the law. The duality of visibility and erasure presents distinct conflict in clearly delineating a pathway forward.

This chapter shows that contemporary educational policies mobilize disgust to discipline queer and trans bodies—recasting their visibility as a threat and their erasure as a moral imperative. Understanding these logics is crucial not only to resisting institutionalized queerphobia but to building schools where all students can exist safely, be recognized in their full humanity, and imagine futures beyond the State's narrow prescription.

Moral Themes and Disgust

Children absorb pro-social messages not just from the people around them, but also the stories and media they absorb. Pro-social messages promote fairness, caring for others, and attentiveness to others' needs. Children understand fairness, but their ability to adopt different peoples' perspectives varies. A study of how children understood pro-social messages in the TV show, *Arthur*, found that children between 4 and 6 years old may not fully understand the message of the episodes, but were able to understand the importance of being kind toward others.[29] Early childhood exposure to media that promotes pro-social attitudes toward LGBTQ+ people may contribute to children being able to empathize and act kindly regarding people with differing gender and sexuality identities than themselves. The successful efforts to ban elementary school-aged children from encountering these materials in the classroom, legitimizes the sentiment that queerness is Other, and contributes to the enshrinement of disgust in law.

Martha Nussbaum writes that LGBTQ+ people are commonly understood as a threat to the body politic due to their presenting radical departures from societal norms, which are built upon cisgender heterosexual patriarchal conceptions of the family.[30] For this reason, queer people are often positioned as distinct threats to children. Project 2025, the presidential transition plan for President Donald Trump created by the conservative think tank the Heritage Foundation and joined by nearly 100 other organizations has pointedly addressed the LGBTQ+ community and its place in public life. The report calls for dismantling "the bullying LGBTQ+ agenda." It goes on to call for the removal of President Biden's 2022 Gender Policy and in doing so pointedly calls for the removal of language pertaining to gender and sexuality from all policies, grants, and programs:

> It should remove all references, examples, definitions, photos, and language…that include the following terms: "gender," "gender equality," "gender equity," "gender diverse individuals," "gender aware," "gender sensitive," etc. It should also remove references to "abortion," "reproductive health," and "sexual and reproductive rights" and controversial sexual education materials. In the past, the word "gender" was a polite alternative to the word "sex" or term "biological sex." The Left has commandeered the term "gender," which used to mean either "male" or "female," to include a spectrum of others who are seeking to alter biological and societal sexual norms. The promotion of gender radicalism is anathema to the traditional norms of many societies…[31]

Project 2025's goals have found their success in the proliferation of the "Don't Say Gay" bills, modeled after Florida's HB 1557, in which LGBTQ+ inclusive curriculum and accompanying bans on child and young adult books with queer characters.[32] These measures, which erase queer people, have the side effect of also making queer people hypervisible. The legal attempt to ban drag performance in both Texas and Tennessee utilized broad language, in which the listed, "topless dancers, go-go dancers, exotic dancers, strippers, male or female impersonators," are within the same category, despite the significant variations between the performers.[33] Not all drag performers include toplessness or stripping. Drag Queen Story House is a popular program, in which drag queens read children's books in public spaces, often libraries, schools, and bookstores.[34] Despite the public accessibility of these events, the myth that these events are sexual and that the queer community is hyper-sexual has been a mobilizing rhetoric behind these bans.

The legal attacks on positive queer visibility harken back to the demonization of LGBTQ+ people from the 1950s of the 1970s. Anita Bryant, entertainer and spokeswoman for Florida orange juice campaign as well as anti-LGBTQ+ rights activist, lays out the anxieties of queerness in public education, "Admitted homosexual teachers could encourage homosexuality by inducing pupils into looking upon it as an acceptable lifestyle. A particularly deviant-minded teacher could sexually molest children."[35] She helped to perpetuate the belief that gay community "recruits" through education, "since homosexual cannot reproduce, they must freshen their ranks."[36] Bryant's position would go on to be adopted and further through legislation attempts to ban homosexuals from public education, such as California's Proposition 6, which would go on to be defeated. The current legislative assaults on public education align queerness with child abuse, the narrative that school teachers are "grooming" children appeals directly to Bryant's own claims in the 1960s and 1970s. Lee Edelman writes, "This, of course, is the connection on which Anita Bryant played so cannily when she campaigned in Florida against gay civil rights under the banner of 'Save Our Children,' and it remains the connection on which the national crusade against gay marriage rests its case."[37]

Public education is a space in which parents entrust their children to be educated not just in content, but also in social mores. Teachers assist their students in social and emotional education, which involves cultivating the innate sense of empathy that all children have. The opportunity for students to engage with LGBTQ+ inclusive curriculum has triggered a new lavender scare and has significant risk for LGBTQ+ youth. School-age queer youth report higher than average levels of depression, anxiety, and suicidality. The Trevor Project's 2024 US National Survey found that queer youth in the age range of 13–24 are at significantly higher rates of suicide risk than non-queer youth.[38] That risk is caused in part by heightened stigma directed toward queer people. The survey further found that roughly 90% of queer youth reported their wellbeing as negatively impacted due to contemporary politics. Nearly half of transgender and nonbinary youth reported considering moving with their family to another State due to anti-LGBTQ+ policies.[39] The codification of disgust distinctly harms queer youth.

Queerness, Disgust, and the Symbol of the Child

Courts have repeatedly upheld the authority of schools to censor or restrict student speech—particularly when that speech challenges dominant norms around gender and sexuality.[40] In *Hazelwood School District v. Kuhlmeier*, the Supreme Court held that schools could constitutionally remove student newspaper content discussing divorce and teen pregnancy, reinforcing the role of schools as sites of moral gatekeeping where students' expressive rights are subordinate to the institutional mission of discipline and norm production.[41]

Disgust, in this context, functions as a powerful regulatory emotion. Although such a framework may seem neutral, it has been disproportionately applied to expressions of queerness, which are often construed as obscene precisely because they unsettle heteronormative ideals. The law, then, becomes a vehicle not only for censorship, but for encoding disgust as a legitimate basis for exclusion.

It ought to be recognized that the form of disgust has a specific moral character to it. Nussbaum, Paul Rozin, Jonathan Haidt, and Clark McCauley describe disgust as something that affirms our unique humanity, and that provides us with a sense of civilization.[42] However, this form of disgust, while civilizing, can also be dangerous and divisive.

Michael Hauskeller defines moral disgust as, "the kind of disgust we experience when witnessing an action or event that immediately, and without further reflection, strikes us as terribly wrong, that is, as something that simply ought not to happen, no matter what the circumstances."[43] The arguments made in favor of "Don't Say Gay" laws regularly appeal to fear, pointing toward myths of child sexual predation and violence as well as public displays of sexuality. By connecting queerness with disgusting behavior, such as child sexual predation, the appeals draw upon our sense of moral disgust, which when rightfully deployed, can help to protect children, and when incorrectly deployed, can stigmatize an entire segment of the population.

Indeed, the current wave of "Don't Say Gay" laws is not an anomaly but the latest iteration of this disciplinary and affective regime. Despite the assertion by legal scholars that "anti-gay curriculum laws are anachronistic—remnants of a time in which governmental discrimination against LGBT people was lawful and rampant," the contemporary political landscape illustrates that these laws are not just modern echoes of the Reagan-era "No Promo Homo" statutes, but the continuation and evolution of such laws in an effort to continue to regulate normative family structures, sexualities, and bodies.[44]

In fact, "No Promo Homo" laws are still on the books in some states. These laws prohibit any positive or neutral discussion of homosexuality in schools, thereby "rendering LGBT people unspeakable" within public education. As Hunter Foist notes, these laws "chill protected speech" and "hinder public health outcomes" by criminalizing acknowledgment of queer existence. Even after *Lawrence v. Texas* invalidated sodomy laws, states like Alabama and Texas continued to mandate that sex education teach homosexuality as "criminal," embedding queerphobia into curricular frameworks that remain in place to this day.[45]

When children are raised in environments where sex is taught as fixed and immutable and heterosexuality is framed as both natural and moral, they are interpellated into a system that, as Judith Butler explains, demands "the compulsory appropriation and identification with those normative demands."[46] These norms are not benign; they are enforced through policies that regulate whose identities can be named, whose relationships can be legitimized, and whose lives are rendered deviant.

This is where the queer child becomes central.[47] The child, as a symbol of the future, must be protected from queerness in order to preserve a particular vision of social reproduction:

> For politics, however radical the means by which specific constituencies attempt to produce a more desirable social order, remains, at itscore, conservative insofar as it works to *affirm* a structure, to *authenticate* social order, which it then intends to transmit to the future in the form of its inner Child. That Child remains the perpetual horizon of every acknowledged politics, the fantasmatic beneficiary of every political intervention.[48]

Thus, laws that prohibit the discussion of LGBTQ+ identities do not merely silence; they invest in a future from which queerness is absent.

Edelman's *No Future* critiques the temporal investment in the heteronormative child as the horizon of political meaning, arguing that queerness is structurally cast as a threat to the future.[49] "Don't Say Gay" laws function as legal reifications of this logic by foreclosing the presence of queerness in educational spaces.

This foreclosure extends beyond silencing; it is enforced through disciplinary mechanisms like forced outing policies. For example, many of the same states that have "Don't Say Gay" laws also enforce forced outing policies, which require school staff to disclose a transgender student's gender identity to parents if the student requests to use a chosen name or different pronouns.[50] Outing in this context is not merely a form of surveillance but a disciplinary act—regulating gendered subjectivity through the threat of exposure, familial correction, and institutional control. These policies reassert parental authority, restore heteronormative coherence, and punish deviations from State-sanctioned identity formations. In doing so, they compel a return to the normative family structure, treating the queer child as both a threat to and a disruption of the imagined continuity of the social order.

Such laws are animated, in part, by a culturally sanctioned disgust of queerness—an affect that marks queer and trans embodiment as contaminating, inappropriate, or obscene. This is rendered most legible in the recent moral panic over LGBTQ+ books in school libraries—where queer texts like *Gender Queer* are labeled "pornographic"—further reveals how disgust is deployed as a tool of censorship and cultural erasure.

The disgust directed toward queer people is illustrative of shame.[51] Eve Sedgwick writes about shame in *Touching, Feeling*:

> Shame interests me politically, then, because it generates and legitimates the place of identity—the question of identity—at the origin of the impulse to the performative, but does so without giving that identity space the standing of an essence. It constitutes it as to-be-constituted, which is also to say, as already there for the (necessary, productive) misconstrual and misrecognition. Shame—living, as it does, on and in the muscles and capillaries of the face—seems to be uniquely contagious from one person to another. And the contagiousness of shame is only facilitated by its anamorphic, protean susceptibility to new expressive grammars.[52]

Shame is an internalization of some insecurity and feeling of difference. Sex and gender are categories of being that can inspire insecurity. The lack of control, particularly in how others perceive *you* lead to a need to feel some sort of control, and one way in which to do so is to establish *you* as "normal" and others as "deviant." The deviants must then conceal themselves so as to preserve your own comfort. This form of scapegoating queer people in particular reveals an underlying social insecurity and anxiety toward queer people who trouble ideas of how one ought to behave and live publicly and privately. By erasing queer people from popular culture, they then are removed from public consciousness, a type of public death.

The State has not only a biopolitical aim, but also a necropolitical aim in regulating LGBTQ+ people. Necropolitics, as defined by Achille Mbembe, is the State's "capacity to dictate who may live and who must die."[53] Expanded upon by queer theorists, queer necropolitics explores, "a range of spectacular and mundane forms of killing and of 'letting die'."[54] In this context, the public erasure of queerness operates not only as symbolic death but as a mechanism of control that structures who is allowed to appear, to speak, and ultimately, to be protected. As queer theorists explain, schools are embedded within what Mbembe calls "topographies of cruelty" and operate as sites of "necropolitical spatialities."[55] In this context, educational censorship becomes one of the State's tools for rendering queer life unintelligible, undeserving of recognition, or even existence.

In one instance, one of the books banned by a Florida school district in compliance with the State's "Don't Say Gay" law was *And Tango Makes Three* tells the true story of two male penguins who form a pair bond and raise a chick together. "If *And Tango Makes Three* does not contain sexual content, why is it being removed from classroom libraries and media centers? The short answer is simple: Florida is seeking to suppress the idea that queer people exist," explained Foist. "Even though same-sex couples are not uncommon among penguins, Florida's government sees their very existence as a threat. This book about real penguins is not sexual. It is not 'pornographic.' It is not 'developmentally inappropriate.' It is queer. And that is enough for Florida to decide that it cannot remain on classroom bookshelves."[56]

As Foist illustrates, proponents of "Don't Say Gay" legislation often claim their aim is merely to give parents more control or to remove "pornographic" material from schools.[57] But the data tells a different story. In 2020, over half of the top twenty most banned books featured queer storylines—even when those books included no mention or depiction of sexual content.[58] As legal scholar Todd Pettys notes, these bans reflect a misapplication of obscenity laws. The First Amendment protects materials with "serious literary, artistic, political, or scientific value"—a standard that many of these works clearly meet.[59] "If public and private actors believe these books are harmful to children, they must deploy tools other than state and federal obscenity laws," Pettys explains.[60] What is being targeted, then, is not obscenity but deviance.

At the same time, these laws have very real, present-tense effects. Laws that restrict discussion of LGBTQ+ identities in schools—such as "No Promo Homo" policies and their modern counterparts like "Don't Say Gay" laws—have had a profoundly negative impact on LGBTQ+ youth. Research from GLSEN shows that students living in states with these restrictive laws are more likely to experience a hostile school climate.[61] They report fewer supportive peers who accept LGBTQ+ identities, hear homophobic language more often, and face higher rates of bullying, harassment, and even assault based on their sexual orientation or gender expression.[62] Research also shows that transgender and nonbinary youth who were involuntarily outed were more likely to face severe depression and reported feeling less supported by their families than those whose identities remained private.[63]

Other discriminatory laws, such as bathroom bans, do more than deny students access to basic facilities—they function as technologies of power that regulate how bodies are permitted to move through space, determining who is entitled to safety and privacy. These bans operate through disciplinary mechanisms that mark certain bodies—particularly queer, trans, and non-normative ones—as threats to the social order, rendering them hyper-visible, surveilled, and punishable.[64]

By controlling access to space, these policies do not merely reflect societal norms; they actively produce and enforce them. They criminalize deviance not because it exists inherently, but because power requires it to. In this way, the law participates in the construction of the very subjects it seeks to regulate.[65] These policies reinforce the notion that public space belongs only to those whose bodies do not disturb its normative contours, while pathologizing those who refuse—or are unable—to conform.

According to a 2022 study by the Trevor Project, 91% of transgender and nonbinary youth (TGNB) expressed concern that laws at the State or local level might restrict transgender people from using bathrooms that match their gender identity. Another study published in the *Journal of*

Adolescent Health found that 58% of TGNB youth surveyed had been blocked or discouraged from using bathrooms that aligned with their gender identity.[66] Among those who experienced such discrimination, 85% reported symptoms of depression, and 60% had seriously considered suicide.[67] One in three reported a suicide attempt in the past year, and one in five had attempted multiple times.[68]

These statistics are not just numbers—they reflect the material consequences of a legal and cultural order that renders trans lives disposable. The case of Nex Benedict, an Indigenous trans student who died after being assaulted in a school bathroom, exemplifies the fatal convergence of State-sanctioned transphobia, racialized violence, and institutional neglect.[69]

These findings reaffirm frequent arguments made by queer people—that negative messaging surrounding queerness has material negative impacts. Studies repeatedly find that LGBTQ+ youth who have supportive families, experience better mental health and are less likely to experience substance abuse and have better stress-coping mechanisms.[70] Expansions of support for LGBTQ+ youth to the community outside of their family likewise positively contributes to their mental health and long-term wellbeing.

The direct penalization and neglect of queerness is a rejection of personal *and* institutional responsibility for care. Joan Tronto argues that within a caring democracy, *all* citizens, and presumably the State itself, have a responsibility to care.[71] Yet, this responsibility is frequently eschewed, or placed upon the individual themselves. Responsibility is less clear, than a notion of rights. It often corresponds to a duty or a moral obligation between individuals interpersonally, and as political obligations. If we believe the State has an obligation to ensure an inclusive public education, we are making a political claim. Tronto argues that responsibility is a necessary component of care ethics. We are responsible to one another due to some moral social networks, and thus the neglect of LGBTQ+ youth calls for an investigation into responsibility.

Authors of "Don't Say Gay" bills and Project 2025 interpret queerness itself as a threat to the moral order. If a group of people are a threat, do we still have an obligation to those people? The claims of deviance have, as we discussed, been a tool to remove persons from political and public life. These claims also are ways to legally enshrine *irresponsibility*. Tronto establishes three ways of cementing irresponsibility:

> A first way to avoid responsibility is through ignorance. Not knowing about a problem seemingly absolves one from trying to solve it. A second way to avoid responsibility is to create an institutional structure that deliberately diffuses and obscures lines of authority...Another source of such irresponsibilities is the kinds of political, social, economic, and cultural decisions that operate in the background.[72]

The legal efforts to erase queer people, while simultaneously rendering them hyper-visible, indicates that this current form of irresponsibleness is thoughtful. It is not ignorant. The law is actively articulating false ideas of queer people, thereby making them *known* through these articulations. Ultimately, the law appeals to the court's authority. The line of authority is not in question. Tronto's third method of obfuscation is particularly salient. It is the right-wing cisgender heterosexual patriarchal interpretations of the world and the moral order that justify the profound lack of care regarding queer youth.

Care is always personal, and as a result, differences matter. Within the current political paradigm, these differences are utilized to not only divide queer people from the body politic, but to also exclude them from discourse through labeling them as deviant. Difference does not have to operate in such a manner. Difference can, in fact, bring communities together through curiosity.

Curiosity is frequently associated with children or childhood, terms like "child-like curiosity" are often employed to laud adults who are interested in vastly different areas of knowledge. Curiosity spikes our interest in others' lives and others' experiences. While we all share the essential human condition of vulnerability and to some degree have similar experiences, we will never have the full capacity to understand another's life. Ludwig Wittgenstein in *Philosophical Investigation* agonizes over how we understand if *our* definition of pain is the same as someone else's.[73] This drive to understand the world necessarily includes building relationships with others; Martha Nussbaum names relationships as one of the capabilities that must be met in order to have a meaningful life. Care necessitates some level of interest in others, and this interest arises most frequently due to our dissimilarities. Difference contributes to not just a richer society, but a richer moral and ethical political development.

Conclusion

As schools are used to regulate bodies and possibilities and reify fearful and violent images of queer sexual predators, we find ourselves in a tenuous moment. Visibility, here as with disability, is simultaneously a tool to combat discriminatory attitudes and prejudices and a weapon of the State. However, if we reframe visibility through the lens of care, and its required characteristics and attitudes, then visibility can operate as a liberatory tool, one which affirms our responsibility to one another and encourages curiosity.

LGBTQ+ people matter due to their personhood. They have inherent moral worth that exists outside of their sexual and gender identities and orientations. The disgust which is turned toward queer people is frequently framed in terms of moral and social norm-breaking. However, moral disgust, that sentiment which compels us to identify something which can *never* be supported, is unsupportable when it is applied to difference. Difference itself is an assumed category of Being, one that is an innate part of our experience. Each person experiences their gender and sexuality differently, even if they hold the same gender and sexual identity and orientation. By virtue of their difference, their experiences are in turn different. It is unthinkable to categorize a shared human quality as divergent or threatening. In the same way, our shared vulnerabilities ought not to be thought of as threatening.

Difference and vulnerability become threatening to the larger liberal legal theories when considered in terms of collectivity. Once our differences are thought of as collective bonds, rather than things that separate us, and as essential to our shared obligations toward one another, these differences bind us together in much the same way the disability forward framework binds us through our vulnerabilities. Care is always assessed within the context of a particular person in a particular situation. Care always is attuned for difference. Likewise, in drawing our attention to difference, we also find ourselves aware of what things we share. If we highlight queerness as a way of Being, we may then find ourselves alerted to other possible ways of Being or even ways in which people who may not identify as LGBTQ+ may be living queerly.

Ultimately, these regulatory practices must be read not just as legal or educational disputes but as part of a broader apparatus of control. They are attempts to discipline queer bodies, foreclose queer futures, and solidify a normative order through the production of docile, heterosexual, and binary-gendered subjects. In this sense, the school is not a neutral ground but a battleground—where disgust becomes law, where the First Amendment is weaponized against those it was meant to protect, and where queer survival hangs in the balance.

Notes

1. Sham Habteselasse and Sam LaFrance, "What Students Lose When School Becomes a Political Battleground," *American Civil Liberties Union*, February 20, 2025. https://www.aclu.org/news/free-speech/what-students-lose-when-school-becomes-a-political-battleground.
2. Movement Advancement Project, "The State of Schools for Trans Youth in 2025," Medium, February 25, 2025, https://lgbtmap.medium.com/the-state-of-schools-for-trans-youth-in-2025-6110a86b3cb7.
3. Gaia Ballatori, "Knowledge Control as a Form of Social Control: From Hermeneutical Injustice to Epistemology of Resistance," *Astrolabio* 26 (2022): 48.
4. *Bethel Sch. Dist. v. Fraser*, 478 U.S. 675, 677.
5. Jojanneke van der Toorn, Ruthie Pliskin, and Thekla Morgenroth, "Not Quite Over the Rainbow: The Unrelenting and Insidious Nature of Heteronormative Ideology," *Current Opinion in Psychology* 46(2022): 101,340, https://doi.org/10.1016/j.copsyc.2022.101340.
6. See Lee Edelman, *No Future: Queer Theory and the Death Drive* (Durham, NC: Duke University Press, 2004).
7. Judith Butler, *Bodies That Matter: On the Discursive Limits of Sex* (New York: Routledge, 1993), x.
8. Eve Kosofsky Sedgwick, *Epistemology of the Closet* (Berkeley: University of California Press, 1990), 73.
9. Ibid., 70.
10. Ibid., 63.
11. Movement Advancement Project, "Bans on Transgender Youth Participation in Sports," Accessed March 30, 2025. https://www.lgbtmap.org/equality-maps/youth/sports_participation_bans.
12. Movement Advancement Project, "Bans on Transgender People Using Public Bathrooms and Facilities According to Their Gender

Identity," Accessed March 30, 2025. https://www.lgbtmap.org/equality-maps/youth/school_bathroom_bans.

13. See Dean Spade, "Rethinking Transphobia and Power—Beyond a Rights Framework." In *Normal Life: Administrative Violence, Critical Trans Politics, and the Limits of Law*, 50–72. Revised and Expanded Edition (Durham, NC: Duke University Press, 2015).
14. Movement Advancement Project, "Forced Outing of Transgender Youth in Schools," Accessed March 30, 2025. https://www.lgbtmap.org/equality-maps/youth/forced_outing.
15. Article: *School Pronoun Rules and the Compelled-Speech Objection,* 75 Mercer L. Rev. 579, 580.
16. Mia Fischer, *Terrorizing Gender: Transgender Visibility and the Surveillance Practices of the U.S. Security State* (Lincoln: University of Nebraska Press, 2019), 170.
17. Margot Canaday, *The Straight State: Sexuality and Citizenship in Twentieth-Century America* (Princeton, NJ: Princeton University Press, 2009), 2.
18. The Trevor Project, "Anti-Transgender Laws Cause up to 72% Increase in Suicide Attempts Among Transgender and Nonbinary Youth, Study Shows," September 26, 2024. https://www.thetrevorproject.org/blog/anti-transgender-laws-cause-up-to-72-increase-in-suicide-attempts-among-transgender-and-nonbinary-youth-study-shows/.
19. Movement Advancement Project, "Under Fire: New MAP Report Details Eight Tactics to Erase LGBTQ People from Schools and Public Life," March 23, 2023. https://www.mapresearch.org/news/2023-press-release-under-fire-report-2.
20. See Fla. Stat. § 1000.071.
21. Eesha Pendharkar, "Florida Just Expanded the 'Don't Say Gay' Law. Here's What You Need to Know," *Education Week*, April 19, 2023. https://www.edweek.org/policy-politics/florida-just-expanded-the-dont-say-gay-law-heres-what-you-need-to-know/2023/04.
22. Movement Advancement Project, "LGBTQ Curricular Laws," Accessed March 30, 2025. https://www.lgbtmap.org/equality-maps/curricular_laws.
23. Hunter Foist, "Keep Saying Gay: How Nationwide" Don't Say Gay" Bills Violate the First Amendment, Chill Protected Speech,

and Hinder Public Health Outcomes," *Ind. Health L. Rev.* 21 (2024): 177.

24. Jo Yurcada, and Jay Valle, "Republicans Introduce National 'Don't Say Gay' Bill to Restrict LGBTQ Discussions in Schools," *NBC News,* October 19, 2022. https://www.nbcnews.com/nbc-out/out-politics-and-policy/national-dont-say-gay-law-republicans-introduce-bill-restrict-lgbtq-re-rcna53064.
25. Donald J. Trump, "Ending Radical Indoctrination in K-12 Schooling," *The White House*, January 29, 2025. https://www.whitehouse.gov/presidential-actions/2025/01/ending-radical-indoctrination-in-k-12-schooling/.
26. Robin Maril, "Queer Rights After *Dobbs v. Jackson Women's Health Organization,*" *San Diego Law Review* 60(2023): 45.
27. Athina Morris, and Nexstar Media Wire, "Gov. DeSantis Signs Controversial 'Don't Say Gay' Bill into Law," *KGET*, March 28, 2022. https://www.kget.com/national-news/gov-desantis-signs-controversial-dont-say-gay-bill-into-law/amp/.
28. Matt Lavietes, "Florida School Districts Removed Roughly 300 Books Last School Year," *NBC News*, September 12, 2023. https://www.nbcnews.com/nbc-out/out-news/florida-school-districts-removed-roughly-300-books-last-school-year-rcna104367.
29. Darcia Narvaez, Tracy Gleason, Christyan Mitchell, and Jennifer Bentley, "Moral Theme Comprehension in Children," *Journal of Educational Psychology* 91, no.3(1999): 477; Drew P. Cingel, Sindy R. Sumter, and Jiska van de Leur, "The Role of Social Context During Television on Children's Moral Judgements about Social Exclusion and Stigmatization of Others," *Media Psychology* 22, no.1(2019): 133–51.
30. Martha Nussbaum, *Hiding from Humanity,* 113.
31. "Project 2025: Mandate for Leadership, The Conservative Promise," Edt. Paul Dans and Steven Groves, 259.
32. Gisselle Medina, "LGBTQ+ Books Bans are Hitting California Schools," *Los Angeles Times*, August 10, 2023, https://www.latimes.com/california/story/2023-08-10/lgbtq-book-bans-are-hitting-california-schools-how-teachers-can-fight-back; Kevin Rector, "Queer People Have Shaped America," *Los Angeles Times*, June 6, 2024, https://www.latimes.com/california/story/2024-06-06/queer-lgbtq-america-protect-kids.

33. "Tennessee Senate Bill No.3," https://www.capitol.tn.gov/Bills/113/Amend/HA0011.pdf.
34. *Drag Story Hour*, https://www.dragstoryhour.org/.
35. Anita Bryant, *The Anita Bryant Story: The Survival of Our Nation's Families and the Threat of Militant Homosexuality* (Old Tappan, New Jersey: Revell, 1977), 115.
36. Anita Bryant and Bob Green, *At Any Cost* (Old Tappan, New Jersey: Revell, 1978).
37. Lee Edelman, *No Future: Queer Theory and the Death Drive* (Durham, NC: Duke University Press, 2004), 19.
38. "2024 U.S. National Survey on the Mental Health of LGBTQ+ Young People," *The Trevor Project*, https://www.legis.state.pa.us/WU01/LI/TR/Transcripts/1995_0089_0011_TSTMNY.pdf.
39. Ibid.
40. See *Bethel Sch. Dist. No. 403 v. Fraser*, 478 U.S. 675 (1986) and *Evans-Marshall v. Bd. of Educ. of Tipp City Exempted Vill. Sch. Dist.* 624 F.3d 332 (6th Cir. 2010); and *Ochshorn ex rel. v. Ithaca City Sch. Dist.*, 645 F.3d 533, 536 (2d Cir. 2011).
41. 484 U.S. 260 (1988).
42. Martha Nussbaum, *Hiding from Humanity*; Paul Rozin, Jonathan Haidt, and Clark R. McCauley, "Disgust: The Body and Soul Emotion," In *Handbook of Cognition and Emotion,* Ed. T. Dalgleish and M. Power (John Wiley and Sons, 1999), 429–445.
43. Ibid., 599.
44. Clifford Rosky, "Anti-gay Curriculum Laws."*Colum. L. Rev.* 117 (2017): 1461, 1464.
45. John Riley, "Alabama Governor Signs Bill to Remove Anti-Gay Language from Sex Education Curriculum," *Metro Weekly*, April 29, 2021. https://www.metroweekly.com/2021/04/alabama-governor-signs-bill-to-remove-anti-gay-language-from-sex-educat ion-curriculum/.
46. Judith Butler, *Bodies That Matter*, xxi.
47. Eve Kosofsky Sedgwick, *Tendencies* (Durham, NC: Duke University Press, 1993); Lee Edelman, *No Future.*
48. Lee Edelman, *No Future,* 2–3.
49. Ibid, 4.
50. Movement Advancement Project, " LGBTQ Curricular Laws," Accessed April 4, 2025. https://www.lgbtmap.org/equality-maps/curricular_laws; Movement Advancement Project, " Forced

Outing of Transgender Youth in Schools," Accessed April 4, 2025. https://www.lgbtmap.org/equality-maps/youth/forced_outing.

51. Judith Butler, *Bodies That Matter*, 182.
52. Eve Kosofsky Sedgwick, *Touching Feeling: Affect, Pedagogy, Performativity* (Duke University Press, 2003), 64.
53. Achille Mbembe, "Necropolitics." *Public Culture* 15, no. 1 (2003): 11. https://doiorg.du.idm.oclc.org/10.1215/08992363-15-1-11.
54. Jin Haritaworn, Adi Kuntsman, and Silvia Posocco, "Introduction," in *Queer Necropolitics*, ed. Jin Haritaworn, Adi Kuntsman, and Silvia Posocco (Abingdon, Oxon: Routledge, 2014), 4, https://doi.org/10.4324/9780203798300.
55. Ibid, 19.
56. Hunter Foist, "Keep Saying Gay," 177, 192.
57. Ibid, 193.
58. Kaitlin Reilly, Authors of LGBTQ Books For Youth Speak Out About Being Banned: 'Feels Like an Attack Against My Personhood, Because That Is What It Is', (Apr. 12, 2022),https://www.yahoo.com/lifestyle/banned-books-ya-queer-authors-173156815.html.
59. *Miller v. California413 U.S. 15, 24 (1973).*
60. Todd E. Pettys, "Serious Value, Prurient Appeal, and" Obscene" Books in the Hands of Children." *Wm. & Mary Bill Rts. J.* 31 (2022): 1003, 1040.
61. GLSEN, "Laws that Prohibit the 'Promotion of Homosexuality': Impacts and Implications," https://www.glsen.org/sites/default/files/2019-12/No_Promo_Homo_2018.pdf.
62. Ibid.
63. Vincent Gabrielle, "UConn Study: Why Being Outed as LGBTQ Is Bad for Youth Mental Health," *CT Insider*, April 21, 2024. https://www.ctinsider.com/news/article/ct-lgbtq-outed-youth-mental-health-uconn-study-19398381.php.
64. Toby Beauchamp, *Going Stealth: Transgender Politics and U.S. Surveillance Practices* (Durham, NC: Duke University Press, 2019), 100.
65. Judith Butler, *Bodies That Matter*, x.
66. Price-Feeney M, Green AE, Dorison SH. "Impact of Bathroom Discrimination on Mental Health Among Transgender and

Nonbinary Youth. J Adolesc Health." 2021 Jun;68(6):1142–1147. https://doi.org/10.1016/j.jadohealth.2020.11.00.
67. Ibid.
68. Ibid.
69. Desiree Kane, and Jen Byers. "Amid Legacies of Colonial and Anti-Trans Harm, Two-Spirits Struggle for Safety: This Trans Day of Remembrance, We Are Holding Nex Benedict and All Two-Spirit People in Our Hearts," *Truthout*, November 20, 2023.https://truthout.org/articles/amid-legacies-of-colonial-and-anti-trans-harm-two-spirits-struggle-for-safety/.
70. Camille Brown, Carolyn M. Porta, Marla E. Eisenberg, Barbara J. McMorris, and Renee E. Sieving, "Family Relationships and the Health and Well-Being of Transgender and Gender-Diverse Youth: A Critical Review," *LGBT Health* 7, no.8(2020); Stuart Roe, "'Family Support Would Have Been Like Amazing' LGBTQ Youth Experiences with Parental and Family Suppot," *The Family Journal* 25, no.1(2017): 55–62.
71. Joan C. Tronto, *Caring Democracy: Markets, Equality, and Justice* (New York: New York University Press, 2013), 60.
72. Ibid.
73. Gaile Polhaus and John R. Wright, "Using Wittgenstein Critically: A Political Approach to Philosophy," *Political Theory* 30, no.6(2002): 105, 802; Ludwig Wittgenstein, *Philosophical Investigations* (UK: Basic Blackwell, 2009); Riley Clare Valentine, "Their Is No They're: Wittgenstein On Pluralistic Democracy," *Thesis Eleven* 148, no.1(2018): 39–51.

CHAPTER 4

Reproductive Rights and the Revival of the Comstock Act

Abstract Pregnancy is a unique legal topic because pregnancy itself is unique. No other biological process includes the growth and development of a future person. Likewise, no other biological process impacts a person's bodily integrity to such an extent. It is no wonder that abortion is such a fraught subject in the United States. Abortion, within liberal frameworks, pits the pregnant person *against* the potential child, in which the pregnant person is asked to defend their own personhood and rights. If the pregnant person "wins," the fetus "loses." This narrative of rights contributes to a stigmatizing dialogue in which abortion is considered a medical process that will inevitably end in trauma, and through this expresses a bias against individuals who have abortions. The history of abortion in the United States is bound up within the liberal dialogue of rights and questions of personhood, setting the stage for the current debates over legal personhood. This chapter examines pre-during-after legislation on abortion in the United States and examines its language and construction of personhood. Central to this discussion is the concept of the "obscene." Obscenity seems to convey more than a notion of something hidden or sexually explicit; it reflects a tool of power and control, which enables the shaping of bodies and behaviors through patterns of visibility and prohibition. In the case of abortion, its labeling as "obscene" then becomes a part of discipline by which reproductive autonomy has been depicted as deviant and hence bound under strict regulation. This dynamic is highlighted in the revival of the Comstock Act, which utilizes

R. C. Valentine and Z. McNeill, *The Coercive Power of the Law*,
https://doi.org/10.1007/978-3-032-07589-5_4

a broad definition of obscenity to impose a moral and legal framework-one that suppresses reproductive choices by making certain aspects of pregnancy and abortion unspeakable or taboo.

Keywords Pregnancy · Abortion · Obscenity · Discipline · Personhood

Reproductive Right

June 24, 2022, *Roe v. Wade* was officially overturned by *Dobbs v. Jackson Women's Health Organization*. The outcome of the case shocked many people; however, the discussions about the future of reproductive access was a frequent discussion in Southern reproductive justice circles. Before *Dobbs* had ever been filed, Louisiana State University hosted an organization which provided information about how to help newly pregnant students access resources, which ranged from social services for individuals who chose to give birth and keep the child, to adoption, and abortion. The organization informed the attendees to prepare for the eventual overturn of *Roe*, and the reactions ranged from surprise to outrage and to exhaustion. Reproductive justice, both in freedom from pregnancy and freedom to be pregnant, was a significant site of activism in the South since *Roe v. Wade*. Jane Roe was originally from Louisiana. For many people in the Southern United States, *Dobbs* was not a surprise. Before *Dobbs*, abortion access had been steadily decreasing in the South. Louisiana, run by a Democrat governor, passed a constitutional amendment which would immediately ban abortion if *Roe* was overturned before *Dobbs* had reached the Supreme Court. W.E.B DuBois infamously said, "as the South goes, so goes the nation," this has become incredibly apt in the reconfiguring of legal personhood post-*Dobbs*. In the face of Louisiana's trigger bans, judges and lawyers promptly began a legal process to postpone the ban. Louisiana was not the only Southern state where judges and others in positions of power attempted to circumvent trigger bans, Texas is another such State. Even so, it was only a matter of time before the bans were enacted and legal personhood became actively renegotiated to include the unborn.[1]

Pregnancy is a unique legal topic because pregnancy itself is unique. No other biological process includes the growth and development of a future person. Likewise, no other biological process impacts a person's bodily integrity to such an extent. It is no wonder that abortion is such a fraught subject in the United States. Abortion, within liberal frameworks, pits the pregnant person *against* the potential child, in which the pregnant person is asked to defend their own personhood and rights. If the pregnant person "wins," the fetus "loses." Justice Kennedy in *Gonzalez v. Carhart*, points to this logic when arguing that a person may regret their abortion and experience, "severe depression and loss of esteem."[2] There is no proof for this, in fact, long-term studies reveal that people do not regret their abortion.[3] However, this narrative of rights contributes to a stigmatizing dialogue in which abortion is considered a medical process that will inevitably end in trauma, and through this expresses a bias against individuals who have had an abortion. Moreover, pregnancy becomes a punishment, and the relationship between the pregnant person and their fetus is one of coercion rather than choice.

An Overview: The History of Abortion and Anthony Comstock

The rationale of *Dobbs* was that abortion was never considered a fundamental right, and that reproductive rights were not a significant part of legal and medical discourse within the time of the Constitution.[4] Throughout the nineteenth century, trials of "infanticide" consistently relied upon women's reporting. Women who had experience with childbirth - particularly midwives, mothers, and matrons—were given priority when it came to documentation of pregnancy or lack thereof.[5] The concept of "intimate knowledge" was seen as more trustworthy, and women were seen, in this specific venue of knowledge, to be experts. Women were used to investigate the bodies of other women. In this specific legal and medical domain, men's knowledge was less important.[6]

The crime of infanticide itself and abortion are at times used simultaneously. However, in the 1820s, abortion and infanticide were legally treated differently. Infanticide cases were brought against the women, and infanticide was illegal in every State. Abortions were criminalized on a state-by-state basis, and as Felicity M. Turner writes, "If states had legislated against abortion, usually the provider - rather than the person seeking the abortion - was subject to criminal investigation. Providing abortions, rather than procuring abortions, was generally illegal. And those who provided abortions were often men."[7] The medical literature that was being generated at the time on abortion and infanticide was developed solely by men. Although midwives were medical practitioners, women could not be doctors, and therefore their perspectives were locked out of what became established as medical knowledge and what doctors would be trained to understand as true. Midwives and their perspectives may have been welcome in the courts, but soon male doctors would supplant them.

Nineteenth-century medical literature established men as biologically superior to women in all ways. Any expert knowledge that had been understood as based in a woman's gendered experience quickly became seen as inferior to that of men. Women were already not allowed to participate in the legal system as judges, lawyers, or jurors. Thus, women quickly found themselves to be at the mercy of a wholly male courtroom and system. The crime of infanticide and the women who were charged with the crime quickly took on the racist fears of the time. Black women were routinely found guilty of infanticide and were penalized at harsher rates than white women. The penalties shifted as well, with confinement supplanting other judicial measures, forcing women into longer jail sentences than before. Abortion and infanticide became crimes unique to women, and the justice system adopted a punitive role. They needed to reform women who were not acting properly. The men who participated in these acts were largely left alone. The shift in reproductive law to one of punishing women, particularly Black women, left an enduring legacy on American abortion law.[8]

The rise of gynecology was frequently based upon partnerships between medical doctors and schools with slave owners. Gynecology became considered a science due its growing focus in the ante-bellum era on research and experimentation. The literature attempted to be value-neutral; however, Deirdre Cooper Owens notes that "Racial reification occurred in these journals when questions emerged about whether certain diseases, features, and behaviors were endemic to women of African descent…"[9] In mid-April 1850 in Augusta, Georgia, Dr. Paul Eve, a founder of the AMA and one of the South's leading surgeons, met with Mary. Mary was a twenty-year-old married Black woman who was experiencing irregular menstrual cycles as well as vaginal hemorrhaging. Dr. Eve reportedly was not surprised by these symptoms as they were normal for Black women. Mary was diagnosed with cancer and her cancerous uterus was removed and then used by Dr. Charles Meigs, Eve's Northern colleague, in Philadelphia to study uterine cancer.[10] Black women's bodies, and later, poor immigrant women, were seen as exceptional due to their supposed hyper-sexuality and susceptibility to specific gynecological illnesses.

Contemporary abortion restrictions continue to most impact marginalized and over-surveilled populations and "establish[es] a two-tiered system of citizenship, ill-prepared to withstand future legal challenges."[11] The overturning of the constitutional right to an abortion has precipitated a seismic shift in reproductive rights, particularly in the South. This shift cannot be disentangled from the legal and cultural narratives that have long sought to regulate pregnancy, abortion, and contraception. These narratives, steeped in punishment, stigma, and obscenity, are reinforced by the revival of the Comstock Act—a historical mechanism of biopolitical control that entrenches power dynamics while restricting individual autonomy.

In response to the invention of artificial contraceptives, states enacted "obscenity" laws criminalizing "obscene" materials and devices to regulate populations by disciplining individual bodies, particularly in matters of sexuality and reproduction.[12] The first criminalization of obscenity in 1815 "triggered a nationwide effort to transform American law and politics through the lens of evangelical Christianity."[13] Even medical professionals were not exempt from prosecution. For example, Charles Knowlton faced repeated charges and hard labor sentences for publishing *Fruits of Philosophy*, a "pathbreaking work" that "attempted to apply science to sexual relations."[14] To evade criminalization, the contraceptive market adopted euphemisms such as "feminine hygiene," "female tonic," "prevention powders," and "Mother's friend."[15]

Anthony Comstock, secretary of the New York Society for the Suppression of Vice, became a prominent enforcer of obscenity laws.[16] In the 1870s, he spearheaded campaigns against saloons, obscene literature, contraceptives, and abortion-inducing drugs.[17] His efforts culminated in the 1873 federal Comstock Act, which criminalized using the US Postal Service to distribute obscenity, contraceptives, and abortifacients.[18] This legislation made the United States the only Western nation to outlaw birth control and established a legal framework to police reproductive health.[19] As Dennis notes in her analysis of obscenity laws, these statutes were less about harm reduction and more about enforcing moral control, disproportionately targeting marginalized populations under the guise of public decency.[20]

In 1878, the Supreme Court affirmed Comstock's power to prosecute lottery dealers under a federal counterpart to the Comstock Act, which prohibited the mailing of lottery materials.[21] The Court ruled that this restriction did not violate free speech, as it merely limited the distribution of such speech. Congress framed materials like obscenity, contraceptives, and gambling communications as "corrupting" and "demoralizing," asserting that laws restricting their distribution via federal mail aligned with First Amendment protections.[22]

By the early 1900s, contraception activist and sex educator Margaret Sanger began challenging anti-contraception laws.[23] In 1914, she coined the term "birth control" and wrote about it in The *Woman Rebel*, her journal, leading to her indictment for nine violations of the Comstock Law.[24] In 1916, she opened America's first birth control clinic in New York, which was raided within ten days by the vice squad.[25] A breakthrough came in 1918 when the New York State Court of Appeals ruled in *People v. Sanger* that physicians could prescribe contraceptives to married patients.[26] Later, in 1936, Sanger led a pivotal legal battle in *U.S. v. One Package* concerning the shipment of diaphragms.[27] The court ruled that physicians could receive contraceptive devices and information through the mail unless prohibited by local law, prompting the American Medical Association to formally recognize birth control as legitimate medical practice.[28]

Anti-abortion rhetoric and legislation frame pregnancy as a moral trial—a necessary consequence of sexual activity. As Priscilla Smith observes, these narrative merge Comstock-era moralism with pseudoscientific claims about the harms of contraception and abortion, cloaking laws rooted in the control of sexual and reproductive autonomy in a veneer of legitimacy.[29] The lasting influence of the Comstock Act, which conflated reproductive health with obscenity, perpetuates the stigmatization of non-procreative sex. Kaplan argues that this devaluation of sexual autonomy reflects an outdated moral hierarchy embedded in obscenity laws, subordinating sexual pleasure and reproductive choice.

Historically, pregnancy has been weaponized as a means of control, particularly against women and other pregnant individuals from marginalized groups, functioning as both a site and a mechanism of State-sanctioned discipline. In contemporary anti-abortion rhetoric and law, pregnancy is framed as a moral trial, transforming the process into a disciplinary ordeal designed to reinforce societal expectations around gender, morality, and reproduction. This framing recasts pregnancy as a form of punitive obligation, where carrying a pregnancy to term becomes both a mandated consequence of sexual activity and an instrument of moral correction.

Reproductive Care Pre and Post-*Dobbs*

The US Supreme Court's decision in *Dobbs* to abolish the constitutional right to abortion astonished legal scholars. Carol Sanger writes in *The Rise and Fall of a Reproductive Right: Dobbs v. Jackson Women's Health Organization* that *Dobbs* raises provoking questions of "What next?" and "How did this happen?".[30] "How could one live (blithely, it now seems) into one's adulthood secure in the highest level of legal protection around reproduction—the constitutional right established in *Roe* and affirmed in *Casey*—only to have it felled with a few determined strokes from Justice Alito's pen in the *Dobbs* case?"[31]

The Supreme Court's "rights reversal" overrules precedent, stripping away from Americans a previously bestowed individual right and endangering other existing freedoms previously affirmed by the court, such as the rights to contraception, intimacy, and marriage equality. To understand the full impact of the *Dobbs* decision on other rights that may be next on the "cutting board," one needs to fully appreciate the legal argument the *Dobbs* court adopted to undermine the rights previously secured in the *Roe*[32] and *Planned Parenthood v. Casey*[33] decisions.

While the Constitution makes no express reference to a right to obtain an abortion, the Supreme Court in *Roe* held that Americans had a right to personal, marital, familial, and sexual privacy,[34] which thus established an American's right to an abortion, as supported by the protections for "liberty" found in the Fourteenth Amendment's Due Process Clause, as well as the First, Fourth, Fifth, and Ninth amendments to the Constitution.[35] In its evaluation, the court in *Roe* reviewed ancient attitudes, the Hippocratic Oath, common law, English statutory law, and the American Medical Association and the American Bar association's positions toward abortion. The court found that the American laws that criminalized and restricted abortion in the United States were of a "relatively recent vintage" derived from statutory changes enacted in the latter half of the nineteenth century.[36]

The *Roe* court then considered the weight of the State's interest, or duty, in protecting prenatal life, finding that, while the State's interest must be balanced with the right of personal privacy:

> The detriment that the State would impose upon the pregnant woman by denying this choice [of whether or not to terminate her pregnancy] altogether is apparent. Specific and direct harm medically diagnosable even in early pregnancy may be involved. Maternity, or additional offspring, may force upon the woman a distressful life and future. Psychological harm may be imminent. Mental and physical health may be taxed by childcare. There is also the distress, for all concerned, associated with the unwanted child...[37]

While the court held that the right of personal privacy includes the right to an abortion, the court determined that right was qualified because of the State's interest. Nonetheless, the court's finding that "a right of personal privacy, or a guarantee of certain areas or zones of privacy [existed] under the Constitution" (specifically in matters relating to marriage,[38] procreation,[39] contraception,[40] family relationships,[41] child rearing and education,[42]) led to "other rights giving individuals control over their bodies and their most personal and intimate associations."[43]

Nineteen years later, the constitutionality of the *Roe* decision was reaffirmed in *Casey*. The decision in *Casey* confirmed the constitutional protection of a person's decision to terminate their pregnancy, as required by the Due Process Clause of the Fourteenth Amendment, which provides that no State shall "deprive any person of life, liberty, or property without due process of law."[44] While *Planned Parenthood v. Casey* upheld *Roe*'s central holding that there is a constitutional right to an abortion, it simultaneously restructured the framework of abortion rights through the undue burden analysis, introducing new mechanisms for State regulation. Rather than reinforcing *Roe*, *Casey* signaled the Court's willingness to accommodate increasing restrictions, allowing for the systematic erosion of reproductive autonomy under the guise of judicial neutrality.[45] This shift was not an anomaly but rather a continuation of a legal trajectory in which the State's interest in controlling reproduction has historically been leveraged against marginalized populations.

Building on this legacy, the Supreme Court in *Dobbs*, held that non-textual rights, or rights that are "not based on explicit constitutional language or deeply-held historical concepts," are not constitutionally protected rights.[46] Per the *Dobbs* court, "the Constitution makes no reference to abortion and no such right is implicitly protected by any constitutional provision, including the one on which the defenders of

Roe and *Casey* ... chiefly rel[ied]—the Due Process Clause of the Fourteenth Amendment."[47] The court argued that historical inquiries are essential when determining the scope of the Fourteenth Amendment's Due Process Clause. The Court held that the right to obtain an abortion was not "deeply rooted in history and tradition," or "essential to our Nation's "scheme of ordered liberty," and therefore was not protected by the Fourteenth Amendment.[48]

Of great importance to the court's ability to undermine the constitutional right to an abortion was the court's finding that a State's regulation of abortion was not subject to heightened constitutional scrutiny. Because the court held that a State's regulation of abortion was not a sex-based classification and that the "'goal of preventing abortion' did not constitute 'invidiously discriminatory animus against women'," the court was able to apply rational basis review, treating the law as a health and safety measure instead of a law protecting individual rights.[49] *Roe*, in many ways, can be considered a promise of individual rights—that people who can become pregnant can and do have a right to exercise their bodily autonomy. While *Dobbs* may often be the case many associate with overturning this promise, previous cases like *Harris v. McRae* had already gutted abortion access for low-income people by upholding the Hyde Amendment, which prohibits federal funding for most abortion services.[50]

In September 1976 Congress began to ban the usage of federal funds to provide abortion. In 1980 the Hyde Amendment took effect; the Amendment states:

> [None] of the funds provided by this joint resolution shall be used to perform abortions except where the life of the mother would be endangered if the fetus were carried to term; or except for such medical procedures necessary for the victims of rape or incest when such rape or incest has been reported promptly to a law enforcement agency or public health service.[51]

When the original Hyde Amendment was passed in 1976, Cora McRae joined a class action lawsuit. McRae was a Medicaid recipient who sought to abort a fetus in the first trimester of pregnancy, which according to *Roe*, was a guaranteed right.

Rhonda Copelon and Sylvia A. Law describe the economic realities of women at the in the 1970s:

> The average cost of first trimester Medicaid-reimbursed abortions in the United States in 1976 was equal to the average monthly welfare payment and more than five times the $48 monthly payment in Mississippi. Testimony from women eligible for Medicaid "established that even under New York's comparatively generous public assistance provision, welfare recipients must live at a miserable and humiliating level of bare subsistence, and that they are without means to pay for abortion."[52]

The district court, and later the Supreme Court were being asked to examine the role of poverty on people's ability to meaningfully access their constitutionally granted rights. The district court originally found that the Amendment was a violation of the Fifth Amendment's Due Process Clause and the First Amendment's Establishment Clause. Once the case was brought to the Supreme Court, the Court examined the case from what Greene has called the "rightist" perspective. Rather than examining the socioeconomic constraints McRae and the other women in the case faced, in which they wanted abortion care, but were not able to afford private healthcare; the Court focused narrowly on the question of funding. Justice Stewart wrote in the Court's decision:

> it does not follow that a woman's freedom of choice carries with it a constitutional entitlement to the financial resources to avail herself of the full range of protected choices. Although the government may not place obstacles in the path of a woman's exercise of her freedom of choice, it need not remove those not of its own creation, and indigency falls within the latter category.[53]

The Equal Protection Clause does not apply to poverty because it is not a category of discrimination. Stewart's decision developed a precedent in which poverty, classism, and the resulting barriers that arise from socioeconomic disparities are outside of discussions on rights, particularly abortion.

Justice Brennan's dissent pointedly addresses the question of poverty:

> The proposition for which these cases stand thus is not that the State is under an affirmative obligation to ensure access to abortions for all who may desire them; it is that the State must refrain from wielding its enormous power and influence in a manner that might burden the pregnant woman's freedom to choose whether to have an abortion. The

> Hyde Amendment's denial of public funds for medically necessary abortions plainly intrudes upon this constitutionally protected decision, for both by design and in effect, it serves to coerce indigent pregnant women to bear children that they would otherwise elect not to have.[54]

Brennan's dissent pointedly considers how limitations on access to abortion are ultimately *coercive*, particularly when these limitations are based along the lines of class. By forcing impoverished people to bear a child, the State articulates a position in which the poor do not have the right to make decisions over reproduction, and instead, ought to bear the consequences for having sex which could result in pregnancy while poor.

These legal constraints on reproductive privacy disproportionately affected those who were already structurally disadvantaged, reinforcing what legal scholar Khiara M. Bridges identifies in *The Poverty of Privacy Rights* as a bifurcated citizenship: one in which poor women, particularly women of color, had a diminished claim to privacy and bodily autonomy in comparison to their wealthier counterparts.[55] In *A Travesty of Justice: Revisiting Harris v. McRae* (2014), Jill E. Adams and Jessica Arons argued that *McRae* was wrongly decided and should be overturned, reflecting a lingering optimism that legal redress might restore and expand *Roe*'s protections. Yet, in light of *Dobbs*, this optimism appears misplaced—not merely because the Court's composition has shifted, but because the legal foundation of abortion rights was always precarious, entangled in a framework that privileged economic status and whiteness as the default for legal personhood.

As of the writing of the book, 41 states have adopted some measure of abortion bans.[56] 28 states have abortion bans based on gestational duration. For example, Florida has restricted abortion access as early as 6 weeks into pregnancy.[57] This has effectively removed people's ability to access abortion in the South. State abortion restrictions have contributed to the United States having one of the highest maternal mortality rates among developed nations.[58] According to a study published in the *American Journal of Preventive Medicine*, states with abortion restrictions suffer a 16 percent increase in infant mortality rate.[59] This research supports prior findings indicating that abortion restrictions correlate with higher rates of maternal and infant mortality, which disproportionately affect Black communities.[60] While many State abortion bans include "exceptions" for life-threatening pregnancy complications, some hospitals have refused to provide emergency abortion care in fear of facing prosecution.

The ethical concerns extend to larger systemic inequities which impact the populations of individuals who seek out abortions. Within the United States, overwhelmingly these populations are already at risk. CDC data and PEW Research, obtained from the District of Columbia and 46 other participating states, report that the majority of abortion seekers (57%) were in their 20s, 87% were unmarried, and 57% had not had a previous abortion. Additionally, "In the District of Columbia, New York City (but not the rest of New York) and the 31 states that reported racial and ethnic data on abortion to the CDC, 42% of all women who had abortions in 2021 were non-Hispanic Black, while 30% were non-Hispanic White, 22% were Hispanic and 6% were of other races."[61] The Guttmacher Institute found that 41% of people obtaining an abortion had an income below the federal poverty level.[62] Diana Foster Greene in a multi-year study of individuals who pursued abortions and were unable to obtain them found that financial hardship is frequently the primary reason for pursuing an abortion. Partner-related concerns and interference with other opportunities such as educational pursuits are also significant reasons for obtaining an abortion.[63] Individuals facing limits on abortion not only experience heightened health risks from risky pregnancies, but also frequently are marginalized groups within the United States and already experience hardship. The inability to obtain a medically necessary abortion exacerbates institutional problems such as racism and classism.

Abortion regulations routinely hold pregnant people to a unique standard that obscures the nuances of the reasonings for a person to pursue an abortion. The decision to abort a fetus is bound up by considerations of health, economic concerns, and safety among others. Abortion legislation, beginning with *Roe,* focuses on the right of a person to make private decisions over their body. Lisa Smyth argues, "the emphasis on privacy prevents any consideration of the sociopolitical forces which produce both involuntary pregnancies and calls for abortion access and constrain the 'choices' of different women in different contexts."[64] If a person is unable to obtain enough funds for an abortion in a State with a six week abortion ban, their choice for an abortion may ultimately be functionally nonexistent. Similarly, if someone wants an abortion so as to pursue other ambitions but is in a relationship in which they feel they cannot pursue an abortion, their choice is limited. Our choices are never fully free of our material conditions and our sociopolitical realities. Liberalism is a philosophy of self-determination and autonomy; it is above all, a philosophy of choice. Yet, for many people, choices around reproductive healthcare are constrained. If abortion is unchooseable, as Katrina Kimport writes, then pregnant people cannot clarify their desires surrounding their pregnancy. If abortion is chooseable, a person may decide to continue their pregnancy, but either way, their decision would be focused around their agency, their desires, and their circumstances.[65] When abortion is not an option, pregnant people are unable to exercise and experience bodily autonomy, which may or may not lead to an abortion. Ultimately, abortion cannot be thought of solely in terms of individual private choice, as doing so simplifies reproductive care, occluding the complex realities and constraints that existed before and after *Dobbs*.

Abortion is above all a decision concerning relationships, and the encroachment of the law on abortion care offers the law an inroad into coercive relationships. Abortion is, ultimately, a unique medical procedure. Jonathan Herring notes, "As a matter of biology, the pregnant woman and the foetus cannot be neatly divided into two people. There is no clear point at which foetal tissue ends, and the woman's tissue begins. They share fluids and space."[66] Biologically the pregnant person and the fetus are intertwined. The health of the pregnant person greatly impacts the fetus. Furthermore, mortality rates of pregnancy are increasing in states with highly limited abortion access as noted previously. The regulations of abortion frequently posit the pregnant person as against the fetus, as though they are two neatly separate beings. The biological inseparability extends to psychological interconnection, in which pregnant people develop significant relationships with the possible child.[67] The experience of pregnancy is profound and is unique, and abortion, in kind, is a medical procedure also profound and unique.

Abortion regulations, such as those in Idaho, posit the relationship between the pregnant person and the fetus as one of conflict. In which, someone who pursues an abortion is ultimately "punishing" or harming a possible child. Despite the overwhelming evidence against this claim, it is at the heart of Idaho's proposed law. It privileges the possible child over the possible parent, ignoring the complexities bound up within that relationship and the decision to have an abortion. It places the law in a curious position in which it mandates a relationship between the pregnant person and the fetus through legal sanctions. The extension of the law to barring EMTALA further instantiates the law in the position of coercing potential relationships. In other words, compelling a patient to continue their pregnancy, enduring potentially life-threatening complications and psychological trauma until they are near enough to "death" for medical intervention, raises significant bioethical concerns as to the role of the law as an arbiter of relationships.

The neoconservative restrictions on abortion articulate a legal perspective long held in the United States, that marginalized minorities' lives and rights are never firmly cemented, but always in a tenuous position. *Dobbs* and the resulting impacts on pregnant people and doctors has not only upended Constitutional law, but also illustrates that the perspective that marginalized people cannot know what is in their best interest is embedded within American law.

Pregnancy as Punishment and the Role of Obscenity and Stigma

Melinda Cooper notes that American legislation surrounding reproductive healthcare as well as sexual health has frequently adopted a moral tone, in which federal aid to people who are sexually active is subsidizing irresponsible lifestyles. She notes that neoconservatives *and* neoliberals oppose abortion access for differing reasons. The former for the belief that the State ultimately will facilitate non-heterosexual patriarchal expression of sexuality. The second from the perspective that if one acts in a risky manner then one is obligated to deal with the consequences, even if the consequences may develop into a human being.[68] Within the United States this debate has resulted in ongoing abortion bans.

The law's punitive stance is especially evident in the enforcement of abortion bans, where pregnant individuals are subjected to burdensome and often insurmountable barriers that position them as subjects of State control. These laws utilize the State as a disciplinary apparatus, compelling pregnant individuals to endure the consequences of biological processes regardless of the profound physical, emotional, or psychological toll involved.

Legal scholar Hilde Lindemann critiques this punitive framework, emphasizing that it subjects pregnant people to an unreasonable standard of bodily sacrifice. Unlike other medical or legal contexts, where personal autonomy is central, pregnancy becomes a condition the individual is compelled to "deal with" in ways dictated by external forces—effectively reducing their agency. Lindemann argues:

> Anti-abortion legislation holds pregnant women -- who are innocent of any wrongdoing -- to a punitive standard of specific performance, sentencing them against their will to the many kinds of hard work, physical discomfort, and outright danger that my daughter willingly undertook to bring her child into this world. No other class of people is held to this standard in peacetime. No woman should be held to it either.[69]

The punitive framing of pregnancy, reinforced by stigma, obscenity, and the revival of the Comstock Act, underscores the intersection of reproductive and legal control as a tool of discipline and moral correction. The overturning of *Roe v. Wade* by *Dobbs v. Jackson Women's Health Organization* has intensified the erosion of reproductive autonomy, particularly in regions already steeped in restrictive legal and cultural narratives. These narratives are not new but part of a broader historical legacy, where laws like the Comstock Act established a precedent for conflating reproductive health with obscenity, stigmatizing non-procreative sexuality, and weaponizing pregnancy as a form of moral punishment.

This legal framework positions pregnancy as a trial of virtue, transforming it into a compulsory burden dictated by societal norms rather than an autonomous choice. As Lindemann argues, this punitive logic imposes an extraordinary and unjustifiable standard of sacrifice upon pregnant individuals, one unmatched in any other area of law or medicine. Such frameworks not only discipline individual bodies but also reinforce broader systems of control, perpetuating societal hierarchies that privilege certain moral and gendered norms over autonomy and agency.

This stigmatization enforces a biopolitical regime in which reproductive decisions are subjected to public scrutiny and legal control. These laws discipline bodies to align with societal ideals of morality and productivity, diminishing individual autonomy in favor of State-imposed norms. Pregnant people, in particular, are positioned as subjects whose bodies are managed and disciplined, reinforcing broader societal hierarchies.

Reproductive law is built upon categories of gender in which cisgender womanhood is the norm. As such, we find patriarchal right-wing interpretations of what it means to be a woman embedded into these punitive perspectives. Martha Nussbaum notes that women's bodies have been labeled as disgusting because they are reminders of vulnerability and physicality particularly through birth and menstruation.[70] Birth makes women interconnected to the continuity of life and thus our animality. Additionally, birth requires semen in some way. Nussbaum argues, "if…semen disgusts males only after it leaves the male body, males will very likely come to view women as contaminated by this (to them) disgusting substance, while the male will view himself as uncontaminated, except insofar as he is in contact with her."[71] Disgust makes us want to separate ourselves from that thing which disgusts us. Thus, laws which limit and regulate women's bodies, as well as others who are found disgusting, rely upon ideologies of power in which these bodies are a threat to the orderliness of society. The decent thing to do, in this framework, is to regulate these bodies and to ensure they do not contaminate society through the public's ability to see and recognize their own vulnerabilities and animality in these bodies.

Reproductive Care as Care

Care involves taking on responsibility and obligations to meet the needs of others. It also ought to include attitudes of respect for the other. Pregnancy is a particular situation in that the pregnant person is largely responsible for the fetus' wellbeing. It is unlike any other situation we have discussed in which there is a level of mutuality and reciprocation. The fetus is a *possible* person, but that is not to deny that there is a relationship of care between the pregnant person and the fetus. People do develop caring relationships with their possible child, particularly as the pregnancy continues. Pregnancy is further unique in that the pregnant person's living conditions directly impact the fetus—such as the pregnant person's access to adequate nutrition. This symbiotic relationship contributes to differentiating pregnancy from any other medical condition or life experience. For this reason, pregnancy ought to be an experience that one opts into willingly, regardless if the pregnancy is intentional or unintentional.

Most people's choices are in some way constrained, and the Supreme Court has reinforced these constraints—particularly in terms of socioeconomic disparities. Decisions such as *McRae* articulate the State's position in which pregnancy is punishment for the poor. We have already discussed the direct impacts of this decision, but this case in particular deserves particular attention in terms of care ethics. Pregnancy is directly mutual in a way most other relationships are not. If a person does not want to be pregnant at that time, and is forced to give birth, their life choices are further constrained, and their relationship with the child may also be impacted. Diane Foster Greene's research finds that ultimately people will develop caring relationships with the child; however, parental bonding is often more delayed than with pregnancies that one has chosen. Additionally, these children have lower child development scores.[72] This is undoubtedly not an optimal condition or outcome for either the child nor the parent. We would hope that once a child is born, it is born into a mutually caring relationship, in which the person who gave birth to them wants that child. Moreover, we would hope that the child is not born under conditions where they face specific medical risks due to parental malnutrition.

Coerced pregnancy, and pregnancies which are negatively impacted by one's class, race, ethnicity, or gender among other such factors, do not meet the conditions of care. The State has a responsibility to exercise compassion and to foster mutually caring relationships. The State, then, has an obligation to support pregnancies that are chosen, and in cases where a person faces distinct burdens, such as malnutrition, the State has an additional obligation to ensure the person's pregnancy is stable. In light of this, we ought to consider, as Herring has argued, that abortion is a public good.

Abortion care, which is chosen and not coerced, supports caring pregnancies. This would allow for meaningful choice. Meaningful choice involves considering broader social conditions that impact pregnancy and abortion. If a person wanted to have a child, but not at this moment, they would be able to safely postpone that decision. Likewise, if a person wanted to have a child, but could not afford to have a child, the State would have a vested interest in the *why* behind these situations. If it were due to the possible child having a disability which the person would not be able to afford adequate care, then expanding care and aid for people with disabilities and their carers ought to be foregrounded. If it were due to the person wanting to finish their education and being concerned over possible student debt, then examining the long-term effects of student debt ought also to be considered. *McRae* ensured that the Courts do not have to consider poverty, which likewise means they do not have to consider other marginalizations which impact decisions over pregnancy and abortion.

Care ethics is a contextual approach which necessitates an examination of decision and choice beyond the rightist arguments in which one either has the right or not. Akin to virtue ethics, what may be caring in one situation may be uncaring in another, such as in the case of Trait Specific Abortions (TSA), in which a person may decide to abort a fetus due to it developing a disability. TSAs reflect positions on disability in which people with disabilities cannot live meaningful lives, nor can they be a positive force in others' lives. Adrienne Asch contends that TSAs exemplify a debate of not *any* child v. not *this* child, in which children with disabilities are unwanted.[73] These forms of abortion reify the liberal conception of personhood, in which the social and political actor is rational, independent, and autonomous. A child and adult with disabilities may lack those capacities, and as such their life is immediately qualified as lesser than those of children and adults without disabilities. Aborting a fetus because of a disability may not be a caring decision, but that does not mean it should be illegal. Rather, it points toward an interrogation of liberal personhood and its impacts on pregnancy and abortion. This language of rights diminishes the dignity of people with disabilities. It reifies ableist conceptions of a meaningful life, support for TSAs, implicitly support reduction in State provisions of care for people with disabilities, as their lives are preventable. If we consider rights in terms of "wins" or "losses" then we lose sight of the overarching concerns of biopolitical and power.[74]

The problem we are consistently confronted with is that people who can become pregnant, particularly racially, ethnically, and economically marginalized people, have never had the same access to reproductive rights as cisgender heterosexual men as well as white cisgender heterosexual middle to upper class women. The moralizing of pregnancy as a punishment for poor choices, including the "choice" of poverty, diminishes the dignity of marginalized persons seeking reproductive care.

Liberalism utilizes the singular "person" as the basis for political thought, but as illustrated with pregnancy there is no singular person. The fetus' life is inextricable from the pregnant person's own. Any legal duties and responsibilities should not be based on observations or theories about generalized fetuses. Rather, we must look to the relationships between the pregnant person, fetus, and their larger community, including society. Herring describes the contextual nature of care and pregnancy as akin to an enmeshed network:

> It flows from this that, for example, the rights and responsibilities that a pregnant woman has would differ greatly in the case where pregnancy was desired and where the pregnancy was unwanted. They might also differ depending on social contexts or the set of personal relationships the pregnant woman was in. The nature of the relationship will affect what

> responsibilities may be imposed upon the community and those close to the woman.[75]

Abortion law ought to be permissive while also reinforcing and supporting the relationship between the pregnant person and the fetus *when wanted*. The purpose of caring reproductive care and caring abortion law is to foster and promote wanted pregnancies, and to assist individuals in terminating unwanted pregnancies. The purpose of this care is to rectify the harm of previous reproductive law which has created tiers of citizenship based upon access to power and privilege, thereby reifying and embedding power structures.

Under the Trump administration, efforts to restrict contraception extended this biopolitical regime, weaponizing reproductive health as a tool of moral discipline. In the middle of Elon Musk's dismantling of the federal government through DOGA, the Trump administration pursued anti-abortion policy. The Department of Justice revived the case over the abortion pill mifepristone, asking to reimpose restrictions that the Biden's DOJ had previously asked a federal judge to dismiss after the Supreme Court ruled that the original plaintiffs were not injured by the FDA's actions pertaining to mifepristone. The attorney generals involved in the case are directly utilizing the Comstock Act's provision against mailing abortive materials.

In addition to the revival of a dismissed case, the Trump administration has dropped out of the case on Idaho's emergency abortions, which the Biden administration had been set to sue, and the administration has asked the Supreme Court for permission to join a case against Planned Parenthood. It is already illegal to use federal funds for abortion care. Nonetheless, South Carolina's governor Henry McCaster has ordered the State's department of health to block Planned Parenthood from Medicaid including for non-abortion services. McCaster claims that *any* abortion provider must be banned from Medicaid because any federal funds will subsidize abortions in some capacity. All of these actions are directly adopted from Project 2025's goal to ban abortion and restrict birth control access.[76]

The active usage of Comstock logic clearly situates American reproductive policy in a federal re-institution of precepts that further subordinated sexual autonomy to State-imposed norms, disproportionately impacting marginalized groups and perpetuating systemic inequities under the guise of moral propriety. Foucault's analysis of biopower highlights how these laws discipline pregnant people to conform to societal ideals of morality and productivity. Pregnancy, in this context, becomes a State-sanctioned tool of discipline, particularly against marginalized groups, transforming it into a punitive obligation that reinforces gendered and racialized hierarchies. Anti-abortion and anti-contraception laws do not merely regulate behavior; they impose a biopolitical order that casts sexual and reproductive autonomy as threats to social cohesion, demanding conformity to a State-defined moral economy. By targeting contraception, abortion, and the "obscene," the far-right is perpetuating a historical pattern of using legal frameworks to control bodies and sexuality. Importantly, non-white people and poor people have been ongoing recipients of these forms of control. The extension of this control to white and middle to upper class people is a significant aspect of the heightened response to these assaults on bodily autonomy. Rooted in the Comstock era's moral governance, these efforts from *Roe* onwards reinforced systems of control that transcend individual autonomy, embedding societal hierarchies and subordinating sexual freedom to State power.

Ultimately, reclaiming autonomy in the face of these punitive frameworks requires confronting the stigmas and power dynamics embedded in obscenity law and reproductive control. By embracing solidarity and transformative legal subversion, there is potential to reframe pregnancy—not as punishment—but as a choice, rooted in dignity and agency. Only then can we begin to dismantle the biopolitical regimes that discipline and regulate bodies, forging a path toward genuine reproductive and sexual justice. The categorization of sexuality as obscene and worthy of punishment presents itself not just in terms of abortion access, but also in the new lavender scare.

NOTES

1. For the purpose of this chapter, we will focus specifically upon people who can become pregnant and the unborn. We use the language of "the unborn" and "fetus" so as to avoid a discussion of early versus late pregnancy and when a possible child becomes endowed with potential rights. There is a rich philosophical discussion on this subject; however, it is not the topic of this book.
2. Supreme Court of the United States, "Gonzalez v. Carhart," 2007, https://supreme.justia.com/cases/federal/us/550/124/. There

is significant scholarship debunking Kennedy's claims; however, it is outside the scope of the paper to delve into that literature; Riley Clare Valentine, "Who has a Meaningful Life: A Care Ethics Analysis of Selective Trait Abortion," *Medicine, Healthcare and Philosophy* (2024): 19.

3. Diana Greene Foster, *The Turnaway Study: Ten Years, a Thousand Women, and the Consequences of Having – or Being Denied – an Abortion* (Simon and Schuster, 2021).
4. *Dobbs v. Jackson Women's Health Org.*, 2247.
5. Felicity M. Turner, *Proving Pregnancy: Gender, Law, and Medical Knowledge in Nineteenth-century America* (Chapel Hill: University of North Carolina, 2022), 35.
6. See King CR. "Abortion in nineteenth century America: a conflict between women and their physicians." Womens Health Issues. 1992 Spring;2(1):32–9. https://doi.org/10.1016/s1049-3867(05)80135-5. PMID: 1,628,000 and Thompson LM, O'Donnell K. Contemporary Comstockery: Legal Restrictions on Medication Abortion. J Gen Intern Med. 2022 Aug;37(10):2564–2567. https://doi.org/10.1007/s11606-022-07684-1. Epub 2022 Jun 10. PMID: 35,688,997; PMCID: PMC9360382.
7. Ibid., 41.
8. Felicity M. Turner, *Proving Pregnancy*.
9. Deirdre Cooper Owens, *Medical Bondage: Race, Gender, and the Origins of American Gynecology* (The University of Georgia Press, 2017), 19–20.
10. Ibid.
11. Riley Clare Valentine and Zane McNeill, "The Libidinal Law."
12. Anthony Comstock's "Chastity" laws, PBS, https://www.pbs.org/wgbh/americanexperience/features/pill-anthony-comstocks-chastity-laws/#:~:text=These%20laws%20stretched%20back%20almost,lewd%2C%20immoral%20and%20promoted%20promiscuity.&text=The%20driving%20force%20behind%20the,New%20Yorker%20named%20Anthony%20Comstock. (last visited Jun 6, 2024). Massachusetts anti-obscenity law's language read: "Whoever sells, lends, gives away, exhibits, or offers to sell, lend or give away... any drug, medicine, instrument or article whatever for the prevention of conception" shall be punished. ALM GL ch. 272, § 21.

13. Geoffrey R. Stone, "Sex and the First Amendment: The Long and Winding History of Obscenity Law." *First Amend. L. Rev.* 17 (2018): 134, 135.
14. Helen Lefkowitz Horowitz, "Rereading Sex: Battles over Sexual Knowledge and Suppression in Nineteenth-Century America" 5–6.
15. Lauren MacIvor Thompson, "Mother's friend: Birth control in Nineteenth-century America National Museum of Civil War Medicine (2017)," https://www.civilwarmed.org/birth-control/ (last visited Jun 5, 2024).
16. In 1868, the first anti-obscenity statute in New York included a ban on advertisements for any "article or medicine for the prevention of conception or procuring of abortion." N.Y. Sess. Laws § 430 (1868).
17. David M. Rabban, "The Free Speech League, the ACLU, and changing conceptions of free speech in American history." *Stan. L. Rev.* 45 (1992): 47, 56; Haywood Broun and Margaret Leech, *Anthony Comstock, Roundsman of the Lord* (A. & C. Boni, 1927); Anthony Comstock and Robert H. Bremner, *Traps for the Young* (Belknap Press, 1967), 158–67, 184–207.
18. Brandon R. Burnette, "Comstock Act of 1873," The Free Speech Center (2009), https://firstamendment.mtsu.edu/article/comstock-act-of-1873/ (last visited Jun 5, 2024).
19. Anthony Comstock's "Chastity" Laws, PBS: American Experience (n.d.), https://www.pbs.org/wgbh/americanexperience/features/pill-anthony-comstocks-chastity-laws/.
20. Donna I. Dennis, "Obscenity Law and Its Consequences in Mid-nineteeth Century America," *Colum. J. Gender & L.* 16(2007): 43.
21. Cristine Carmody Tilley, "The First Amendment and the Second Sex." *Ariz. L. Rev.* 65 (2023): 161, 174 (citing *Ex parte* Jackson, 96 U.S. 727, 736–37 (1878).
22. Ibid.
23. See John D'Emilio & Estele B. Freedman, *Intimate Matters: A History of Sexuality in America* 243 (1st ed. 1998); Linda Gordon, and Bonnie Mass. "Woman's body, woman's right: A social history of birth control in America." *Science and Society* 42, no. 3 (1978).
24. Malladi Lakshmeeramya, *The people of the state of New York v. Margaret H. Sanger* (1918) Embryo Project Encyclopedia

(2018), https://embryo.asu.edu/pages/people-state-new-york-v-margaret-h-sanger-1918 (last visited Jun 5, 2024).
25. Crystal Raypol, "From Acacia to IUDs: The History of Birth Control in the United States," Healthline, https://www.healthline.com/health/birth-control/history-of-birth-control (last visited Jun 5, 2024).
26. Ibid.
27. Malladi Lakshmeeramya, United States v. One Package of Japanese Pessaries (1936), EMBRYO PROJECT ENCYCLOPEDIA (Aug. 9, 2017), https://embryo.asu.edu/pages/united-states-v-one-package-japanese-pessaries-1936.
28. Facts and ideas from anywhere. Proc (Bayl Univ Med Cent). 2015 Jul;28(3):421–32. https://doi.org/10.1080/08998280.2015.11929297. PMID: 26,130,906; PMCID: PMC4462239.
29. Priscilla J. Smith, "Contraceptive Comstockery: Reasoning from Immorality to Illness in the Twenty-First Century." *Conn. L. Rev.* 47 (2014): 971, 974.
30. Carol Sanger, The Rise and Fall of a Reproductive Right: Dobbs v. Jackson Women's Health Organization, 56 Fam. L. Q. 117, 119 (2023).
31. Ibid.
32. *Roe v. Wade*, 410 U.S. 113.
33. *Planned Parenthood v. Casey*, 505 U.S. 833.
34. *Eisenstadt v. Baird*, 405 U.S. 438 and *Griswold v. Connecticut*, 381 U.S. 479.
35. Ibid.
36. *Roe v. Wade*, 410 U.S. 113, 129.
37. Ibid., 153.
38. *Loving v. Virginia*, 388 U.S. 1.
39. *Skinner v. Oklahoma*, 316 U.S. 535; *Roe v. Wade*, 410 U.S. 113, 152.
40. *Eisenstadt v. Baird*, 405 U.S. 438.
41. *Prince v. Massachusetts*, 321 U.S. 158.
42. *Pierce v. Soc'y of Sisters*, 268 U.S. 510; *Meyer v. Nebraska*, 262 U.S. 390.
43. *Dobbs v. Jackson Women's Health Org*. (Kagan, E., dissenting).
44. U.S. Const. amend. XIV § 1.
45. Khiara M. Bridges, *The Poverty of Privacy Rights* (Stanford University Press, 2017).

46. James G. Hodge Jr, et al., "Curbing Reversals of Non-textual Constitutional Rights," 167, 167–169.
47. *Dobbs v. Jackson Women's Health Org.*, 142 S. Ct. 2228, 2242.
48. *Dobbs v. Jackson Women's Health Org.*, 2235. The court also rejected the appeals in *Casey* to justify abortion through the construction of a broader right to autonomy and to define one's "concept of existence."
49. *Dobbs v. Jackson Women's Health Org.*, 2246.
50. Riley Clare Valentine and Zane McNeill, "The Libidinal Law: Sexuality and Desire in U.S. Legal Embodiment," Subjectivity 31, no.3(2024): 286–305.
51. Pub. L. 96–123, § 109, 93 Stat. 926.
52. Rhonda Copelon and Sylvia Ann Law. "Nearly Allied to Her Right to Be'-Medicaid Funding for Abortion: The Story of *Harris v. McRae*," *WOMENS & THE LAW STORIES* (2010): 207.
53. *Harris v. McRae,* 448 U.S. 297 (1980).
54. Ibid.
55. See Khiara M. Bridges, *The Poverty of Privacy Rights.*
56. "Interactive map: US abortion policies and access after Roe," *Guttmacher Institute*, https://states.guttmacher.org/policies/ (last visited May 2, 2024).
57. Ibid; Seung Min Kim, "Biden blames Trump for Florida's 6-week abortion ban, says women nationwide face Health Crisis," *AP News*, https://apnews.com/article/president-joe-biden-florida-donald-trump-abortion-6b069fd8c14c65236d708b347697f0 (last visited May 2, 2024).
58. Munira Z. Gunja, Evan D. Gumas & Reginald D. Williams, "The U.S. maternal mortality crisis continues to worsen: An international comparison Maternal Mortality Rate in U.S. Worsens," *Commonwealth Fund*, https://www.commonwealthfund.org/blog/2022/us-maternal-mortality-crisis-continues-worsen-international-comparison#:~:text=New%20international%20data%20show%20the,most%20other%20high%2Dincome%20countries. (last visited May 2, 2024).
59. Kendall J. Burdick et al., "Abortion Restrictiveness and Infant Mortality: An Ecologic Study, 2014–2018," https://www.ajpmonline.org/article/S0749-3797(23)00408-7/fulltext (last visited May 2, 2024).

60. Pabayo R, Ehntholt A, Cook DM, Reynolds M, Muennig P, Liu SY. Laws Restricting Access to Abortion Services and Infant Mortality Risk in the United States. Int J Environ Res Public Health. 2020 May 26;17(11):3773. https://doi.org/10.3390/ijerph17113773. PMID: 32,466,506; PMCID: PMC7312072; Eugene Declercq et al., "The U.S. Maternal Health Divide: The limited maternal health services and worse outcomes of states proposing new abortion restrictions Abortion Restrictions Affect Mortality Rate," *Commonwealth Fund*, https://www.commonwealthfund.org/publications/issue-briefs/2022/dec/us-maternal-health-divide-limited-services-worse-outcomes (last visited May 2, 2024).
61. Jeff Diamant, Besheer Mohamed and Rebecca Leppert, "What the Data Says About Abortion in the U.S.," *PEW Research Center*, March 25 2024, https://www.pewresearch.org/short-reads/2024/03/25/what-the-data-says-about-abortion-in-the-us/.
62. "Abortion in the United States," *Guttmacher Institute*, June 2024, https://www.guttmacher.org/fact-sheet/induced-abortion-united-states.
63. Sophia Chae, Sheila Desai, Marjorie Crowll, and Gilda Sedgh, "Reasons Why Women Have Induced Abortions: A Synthesis of Findings from 14 Countries," *Contraception* 96(2017): 235; Diana Greene Foster, *The Turnaway Study*; Sarah Miller, Laura R. Wherry, and Diana Greene Foster, "What Happens After an Abortion Denial? A Review of Results from the Turnaway Study," *AEA Papers and Proceedings*, vol. 110 (2014): 226–230.
64. Lisa Smyth, "Feminism and Abortion Politics: Choice, Rights, and Reproductive Freedom," In *Women's Studies International Forum* 25,no.3(2002): 335–345. Katrina Kimport argues similarly in *No Real Choice: How Culture and Politics Matter for Reproductive Autonomy* (New Jersey: Rutgers University Press, 2022).
65. Katrina Kimport, *No Real Choice*, 150.
66. Jonathan Herring, "Ethics of Care and the Public Good of Abortion." *U. Oxford Hum. Rts. Hub J.* (2019): 10.
67. Anne Morris, "Once Upon a Time in a Hospital... The Cautionary Tale of St George's Health Care NHS Trust v. S, R v. Collins and Others ex parte S [1998] 3 All ER 673." *Feminist L. Stud.* 7 (1999): 75.

68. Melinda Cooper, *Family Values: Between Neoliberalism and the New Social Conservatism* (New York: Zone Books, 2017).
69. Hilde Lindemann, "... But I Could Never Have One": The Abortion Intuition and Moral Luck," *Hypatia* 24, no. 1 (2009): 57.
70. Martha Nussbaum, *Hiding from Humanity: Disgust, Shame, and the Law* (Princeton: Princeton University Press, 2004), 111.
71. Ibid.
72. Diana Greene Foster et al., "Effects of Carrying an Unwanted Pregnancy to Term on Women's Existing Children," *The Journal of Pediatrics* vol. 205 (2019): 183–189.e1. doi:10.1016/j.jpeds.2018.09.026; Diana Greene Foster, *The Turnaway Study: Ten Years, a Thousand Women, and the Consequences of Having—or Being Denied—an Abortion* (Simon and Schuster, 2021).
73. Adrienne Asch, "Prenatal Diagnosis and Selective Abortion: A Challenge to Practice and Policy," *American Journal of Public Health* 89, no. 11 (1999): 1649–1657.
74. Riley Clare Valentine, "Who has a Meaningful Life."
75. Jonathan Herring, *Caring and the Law* (Portland, Oregon: Hart Publishing, 2013), 186.
76. *Project 2025,* https://www.project2025.org/; Susan Rinkunas, "Trump Quietly Made 3 Chilling Moves Against Reproductive Freedom," *Democracy Docket,* March 12, 2025, https://www.democracydocket.com/opinion/trump-quietly-made-3-chilling-moves-against-reproductive-freedom/; Carter Sherman, "Trump Launches Fresh Attacks on US Abortion Rights," *The Guardian,* March 4, 2025, https://www.democracydocket.com/opinion/trump-quietly-made-3-chilling-moves-against-reproductive-freedom/.

CHAPTER 5

Punishing Queerness: Bar Raids, Anti-Sodomy Laws, and Gender-Affirming Care Bans

Abstract LGBTQ+ lives in the United States have always existed under the shadow of laws designed to enforce narrow norms of sexuality and gender. While the early twenty-first century brought some high-profile legal victories, the 2020s have seen a surge in measures targeting queer and trans people—especially transgender healthcare bans and renewed moral policing of queer spaces. This chapter shows that these attacks are not new, but the latest iteration of a longstanding legal project. From anti-sodomy statutes and cross-dressing ordinances to HIV criminalization, "moral character" rules, and the 2025 *Skrmetti* decision, the law has repeatedly adapted its tools to police bodies, discipline gender expression, and stigmatize queer sexuality. The targets and language may change, but the underlying goal remains constant: to define acceptable sexual and gender norms, reward those who conform, and punish those who resist. By tracing this pattern across decades, the chapter reveals how contemporary assaults—often framed as protecting morality, health, or children—extend a persistent State strategy to regulate queer and trans existence, linking the policing of queer bodies to broader struggles over reproductive freedom and bodily autonomy. In response to these patterns, we argue for a political care ethic that prioritizes responsiveness and difference.

Keywords Sexuality · Gender · Anti-sodomy · Cross-dressing · Transgender healthcare bans

R. C. Valentine and Z. McNeill, *The Coercive Power of the Law*, https://doi.org/10.1007/978-3-032-07589-5_5

Pete Buttigieg, President Biden's Transportation Secretary, in a July 28, 2025, interview on *Morning Edition*, stated that transgender people's participation in sports is a question of "fairness."[1] Yet, a study partially funded by the International Olympic Committee, found that transgender women experience several physical disadvantages against cisgender women. Transgender women may have larger lungs and grip strength than cisgender women, but they have a lower maximum rate of oxygen consumption than cisgender women as well as cisgender men.[2] The discourse surrounding "women in sports" is but one aspect of the contemporary attempts to remove and repress transgender and gender-nonconforming people.

In spite of the changes over time in the methods of legal and carceral repression of LGBTQ+ people, symbolic and material effects remain constant: the criminalization of queer behavior, gender expression, sexual acts, and spaces to enforce compulsory heterosexuality and gender normativity under threat of punishment.[3] As explained by Catherine A. Lugg, "Criminal law generally has two goals. The first is to deter socially unacceptable behavior. The second goal is to punish such behavior if it occurs."[4]

Some of the disciplinary tools the State used to regulate sexuality are extremely visible. For example, police raids on gay bars and public bathrooms have historically relied on vague statutes like vagrancy, loitering, and "disorderly conduct."[5] Masquerade or cross-dressing laws—often known as "three-article laws" because people could be arrested if not wearing at least three articles of clothing corresponding to their assigned sex at birth—were used to target trans and gender-nonconforming people's gender expression, including drag performances.[6] Liquor licensing rules, "moral character" clauses, and anti-obscenity laws also gave law enforcement broad discretion to harass and arrest queer patrons and performers.[7] According to Lugg:

> Laws are also part of larger social and political systems, and these all interact...Law and the attendant legal system, working in conjunction with the social and political environments, can serve as powerful panoptics, shaping individuals and their behavior.[8]

These laws were used to target and criminalize LGBTQ+ people by portraying queer sexuality as deviant. In doing so, the law created the idea of the "queer subject" it sought to control. The subject was aberrant, contaminated by its own sexuality, and disgusting due to its body and sexuality. As Alan Hyde explains, "law facilitates the construction and abjection of Others whenever it permits classification and exclusion around issues of sameness."[9] The creation of the "Other" reinforces this abjection, which in turn sustains the legal disciplinary apparatus, creating a self-perpetuating cycle of criminalization and marginalization of queer subjects.[10] This construction of the queer subject by the State not only establishes the legal disciplinary apparatus that regulates the subject—and is reinforced by it—but also shapes the queer subject's sense of identity. In the words of Janet E. Halley, "The legal interpellation or hailing of subjects engages us in generating not only how we present ourselves to others, but how we imagine ourselves as persons. It is inextricably material and symbolic because it materially reconfigures the polis by rearranging how people imagine and present themselves in political engagements."[11]

While certain communities—particularly Black, queer, gender-nonconforming, and sex-worker communities—were disproportionately targeted by these laws, their norm-shaping power lay in their uneven and unpredictable enforcement. As Lugg observes, "all laws regulating consensual sexual behavior have a strong panoptic aspect to them: One never knows where, when, or if these laws might be enforced."[12] Maya Campbell has similarly said that "Criminal law is an enforcement mechanism, a key site for the enforcement of the nation's norms." Therefore, self-regulation in the face of fear of criminalization was one of the main tools used by such laws.[13]

This self-regulation in response to the State's panoptic eye relies not only on visible policing and criminalization of queer communities, but also on the systemic State systems that punish queer and trans people which are rendered invisible. Dean Spade, in *Normal Life: Administrative Violence, Critical Trans Politics, and the Limits of Law*, argues that the focus on individual or intentional discrimination obscures the "norms that govern population management."[14] He points to the daily administration of systems—homeless shelters, prisons, jails, foster care, juvenile punishment, public benefits, immigration, documentation, health insurance, Social Security, driver's licensing, and public bathroom access—that both create and discipline subjects.[15] These legal processes are a form of "power that...distribute[s] life chances [and] works as a key method of control."[16] While the more visible forms of violence—such as bar raids and arresting men in cruising areas[17]—makes this control and policing visible, these mundane daily mechanisms of control are the tools that have normalized such violence.

While the State enforces compulsory heterosexuality through this disciplinary apparatus, it has also built a system into it that permits certain forms of "acceptable" queerness. Therefore, the law not only disciplines those deemed the "bad" kind of queer; it also grants conditional "rights" to the "correct" queer subjects: white, wealthy, and assimilated.[18] These subjects' queerness then becomes a form of normativity, such as homonormativity, in which largely white and wealthy LGBTQ+ people decry that they are the same as cisgender heterosexuals and they want the exact same life embedded into the capitalist State. This form of normativity decries kink and other "non-desirable" communities from public expressions of queerness. As Lugg explains, "American law is distributive, doling out both rewards and sanctions…In turn, the general public takes its cues from the government as to whom is to be honored as well as who is to be shunned, ignored, discriminated against, and not protected from violence."[19] Over the past few decades, so-called legal "victories," from expanded anti-discrimination statutes to hate crime laws, have been celebrated for declaring these subjects "equal" to their heterosexual and cisgender counterparts.[20] Yet these gains are not separate from carceral control—they are one of its mechanisms. By elevating a narrow subset of queer people as worthy of protection, the law simultaneously legitimizes and entrenches the criminalization of those who fall outside this ideal.

As Urvashi Vaid explored in *Virtual Equality: The Mainstreaming of Gay & Lesbian Politics*, "mainstreaming has been at once the goal and the logical consequence of our successes" yet, she explains that "even the advances we have made—like the passage of local civil rights rights ordinances—have proved… vulnerable, revocable, and limited."[21] While Vaid wrote this in 1995, recent events have proven her correct. Since 2022, State legislatures have introduced a record number of anti-LGBTQ+ bills targeting transgender youth in healthcare, sports, identity documentation, and public accommodations.[22] In 2025, Iowa became the first State to completely remove gender identity from its civil rights code, stripping transgender and nonbinary people of protections in employment, housing, and public spaces.[23] These State-level rollbacks have been mirrored and amplified at the federal level, where civil rights laws have been weaponized[24] to erode LGBTQ+ workplace protections[25] and to target schools,[26] hospitals,[27] and blue states[28] for affirming trans people. These escalating attacks are not an aberration but the latest expression of a legal system that has long defined queer and trans existence through exclusion, discipline, and conditional tolerance.

The same legal framework that extends equality to the assimilated also facilitates the surveillance, punishment, and exclusion of queer and transgender people—especially Black, brown, poor, and gender-nonconforming communities. In the words of T. Anasi Wilson, "We are rendered inside of the law, insofar as we are always, already reachable by its disciplinary arm but consistently outside of the reach of the protective powers of jurisprudence."[29] T. Anansi observes that Black death is constantly on display as a means to discipline, surveil, and control—revealing how states wield sociopolitical power over life itself.[30] This dichotomy—between those the State will never protect and those it will always exploit—was long ignored by many white LGBTQ+ organizations, whose embrace of the State's carrot-and-stick approach through hate crime legislation and equal protection lawsuits has been criticized by queer advocates of color for entrenching State power.

In the late 2010s, Black queer and trans activists disrupted pride parades in D.C.,[31] Columbus,[32] Toronto,[33] and Minneapolis[34] to bring attention to police violence against Black communities and the continuing murders of Black trans women. The police arrested many of these activists, with the support of white organizers. In Columbus, Ohio, the white crowd jeered at the protesters and clapped in support of the police arrests of the protesters.[35] The 2017 policing of Black queer protesters at Pride made the division within the LGBTQ+ community visible[36]; the aftermath of *United States v. Skrmetti* [37] in 2025 confirms it, as such strategies have coincided with—and arguably fueled—the expansion of State violence against queer and trans people.[38]

These anti-trans laws, steeped in animus,[39] have been upheld by the courts. *Skrmetti*[40]—which, paradoxically, marked both the peak of representational visibility as the first Supreme Court case argued by an openly transgender attorney and a devastating defeat—cemented the State's power to control trans bodies.[41] The authority to determine who can access life-saving care is biopolitical: it governs an individual's capacity to feel at home in their own body, asserts State control over bodily autonomy, and dictates the "proper" purposes of human bodies. It is part of a broader project that relegates transgender people to survival economies, criminalizes their very existence, and profits from their exploitation while stripping them of access to public life and government benefits.[42] In this sense, the decision is also necropolitical: these laws form part of a larger campaign to erase—and ultimately kill—trans people.[43]

While deeply harmful to trans communities, this is not new; it is simply the latest evolution of laws regulating sexuality, gender expression, and queerness.[44] As the *Skrmetti* dissent explains:

> Individuals whose gender identity diverges from their sex identified at birth (whether labeled as "transgender" at the time or not)... have been subject to a lengthy history of de jure discrimination in the form of cross-dressing bans, police brutality, and anti-sodomy laws.[45]

While the *Skrmetti* dissent frames the decision as a puzzling departure from equal protection principles and a misuse of judicial review, it is more accurately understood as consistent with—rather than contrary to—longstanding patterns. For example, when considering the criminal regulation of queer people, many recall the 1969 Stonewall Uprising or the 1981 Toronto Bathhouse raids. However, similar patterns of State violence persist today.[46] In January 2024, the Washington State Liquor and Cannabis Board (LCB), alongside Seattle's Joint Enforcement Team (JET), conducted unannounced inspections of several gay bars, citing "lewd conduct" violations.[47] In 2025, Houston Mayor John Whitmire took part in early-morning raids of two suspected after-hours clubs, La Zona 45 Bar and Lounge and Los Corrales South.[48] These operations, involving multiple State and local agencies, resulted in around 20 arrests.[49]

Scholars contend that these legal actions on queer and trans communities may reflect the influence of far-right think tanks,[50] a decades-long campaign to capture the courts,[51] and an increasingly authoritarian government.[52] However, the rationale behind *Skremetti* and the heightened surveillance of queer communities and spaces also builds on a deeper legal legacy that has cast queer and trans people as "disgusting." As Senthorun Raj explains:

> Disgust and queerness are tangled together in law. This construction of the "Other" has persisted, even as it evolved to tolerate, or even celebrate, the "right" kind of gay or transgender person. Over the past two centuries, legal rights for LGBTQ people have ebbed and flowed, yet the drive to eliminate the "Other" has remained a consistent throughline in the law's many forms.[53]

With that in mind, we examine how the law has historically been deployed against queer sexuality and gender-nonconforming people as a means of surveillance, criminalization, and coercion—serving the State's broader project of enforcing normative sexualities and advancing its political and social objectives.

Queer as in Filthy

Chief Justice Warren Burger in *Miller v. California* (1973) defined obscenity as something disgusting to the senses, and offensive or disgusting, repulsive, and filthy.[54] He further elaborated on this definition in footnotes, looking carefully at the etymology of obscenity and its connection to disgust. What is obscene, is then disgusting, and more precisely, it has no attributes that can positively contribute to society. According to Burger, the law has a role in protecting the citizens from obscene materials. Certainly, we may agree that some materials ought not to be easily available or perhaps available at all, such as in the case of child pornography. Yet the charge of obscenity has often been raised in arguments surrounding queerness. Stephen Carr was hiding in the Appalachian Trail, when he met Rebecca Wright and Claudia Brenner. He first met Wright in a public bathroom, purportedly asking her for a cigarette, which she denied. Wright went back to her partner, Brenner, and they decided to look for a more private campground. Once they relocated to a private campground they had sex. Carr watched them, shot them, and left the two women for dead. Brenner survived, and Carr argued in court that he had become so disgusted by the sight of the two women having sex that he was driven to murder.[55]

"Disgust follows desire," Raj explains.[56] The belief that queer people are disgusting, particularly expressions of queer sexuality as disgusting, is part of a worldview in which queer people are contaminants. Nussbaum argues that individuals who are seen as disgusting and contaminants are reminders of our animality.[57] Anti-sodomy laws specifically target non-procreative sex, sex which is had explicitly for pleasure, rather than for possible pregnancy.[58]

Queer sexuality, particularly non-procreative sexuality, reminds us that sexual pleasure can be in an end in and of itself. "Acts or bodies that fail to subscribe to this norm are rendered deviant or social contaminants," Raj explains.[59] It is hedonistic, without purpose, a fulfillment of our animalistic desires. "Sex that is deemed 'queer' can attract disparate disgust gestures. From sex in public to buggery in the bedroom, activities that violate a majoritarian (hetero) sexual order have been the subject of considerable penal sanction," Raj contends.[60] This moral framing of queer sex as deviant laid the groundwork for its criminalization, creating a legal architecture that sought not merely to regulate specific acts but to police the very boundaries of acceptable sexuality.

As Michael E. Brewer explains, "In the evolutionary lineage of laws touching the rights and behaviors of gays, sodomy laws form the starting point." [61]Sodomy laws in the United States were rooted in British common law, where acts such as intercourse between men or between a man and an animal were explicitly criminalized as sodomy.[62] However, these laws did not initially reflect a concept of sexual identity but rather targeted particular acts. Until the 1940s, American courts broadly interpreted sodomy statutes to encompass nearly all sexual behavior outside procreative intercourse within heterosexual marriage.[63] Interestingly, while courts held that anal intercourse between a man and a woman constituted sodomy, and that either a man or a woman could be found guilty of sodomy for receiving oral sex, courts and legal theorists generally concluded that sodomy between two women was a legal impossibility.[64] In fact, between 1883 and 1944, there were few cases involving consensual sexual activity between adult men.[65]

However, as the twentieth century progressed and the figure of the "homosexual" emerged as a distinct social and medical identity—shaped in part by sexological concepts like the "sexual invert"—legal definitions of sodomy began to conflate specific acts with the broader pathologization of queer identities.[66] "[A]s society came to recognize gays as an identifiable group, sodomitical acts became more and more identified with homosexuals," Brewer argues.[67] Sodomy criminalization—often prosecuted as lewd conduct or vagrancy—intensified alongside police surveillance of queer communities from the early 1900s through the 1960s.[68] During the Lavender Scare, arrests of LGBTQ+ individuals spiked.[69] In California alone, an estimated 5,000 men were arrested each year for consensual homosexual activity between 1945 and 1965.[70]

Anti-sodomy laws not only criminalized homosexuality but also fueled violence against queer people, deepening marginalization and prompting self-repression within the community.[71] Ryan Goodman has argued that even when sodomy laws aren't enforced they are "an expression of public sentiment (without recognizing that the laws, in fact, also help to generate that sentiment) [which] obscures the complexity of law's dynamic relationship with society and systems of social control."[72] Anti-sodomy laws are frequently called "Crimes Against Nature" laws, and while *Lawrence v. Texas* (2003) rendered these statutes illegal, current anti-queer legislation furthers the perspective that queerness, particularly queer men's sexuality, is disgusting.[73] Nussbaum argues the disgust targeted toward queer men is similar to the disgust experienced by cisgender heterosexual women, who are seen as vehicles for semen, penetrable, and animalistic:

> What inspires disgust is typically the male thought of the male homosexual, imagined as anally penetrable. The idea of semen and feces mixing together inside the body of a male is one of the most disgusting ideas imaginable -- to males, for whom the idea of nonpenetrability is a sacred boundary against stickiness, ooze, and death. The presence of a homosexual male in the neighborhood inspires the thought that one might oneself lose one's clean safeness, become the receptacle for those animal products. Thus disgust is ultimately disgust as one's own imagined penetrability and ooziness, and this is why the male homosexual is both regarded with disgust and viewed with fear as a predator who might make everyone else disgusting.[74]

The queerphobia that queer men experience distinctly focuses upon sex. Queer women may elicit anxiety, hatred, and disgust but their sexuality is frequently fetishized in a way that queer men's is not. Rather queer men embody that which is impure, and therefore their presence, particularly in social roles such as that of an educator, is disturbing and possibly dangerous. Queer people are routinely portrayed as threats to the family and to children. Queer marriage and long-term partnerships outside of marriage present alternative ways to live, without engaging in cisgender heterosexual norms and thereby trouble the normativity of the cisgender heterosexual patriarchal family. These possibilities elude control and agitate fears around cisgender heterosexual normativity as that to which we all ought to aspire to.

Once disgust is acted upon, it is easily enforced through violence. A 2024 survey in California found, "transgender women and men were more likely to have experienced past-year physical violence, while transgender men and nonbinary individuals were more likely to experience past-year sexual violence" than cisgender women and men.[75] In 2022, the FBI recorded over 2,000 hate crimes directed toward LGBTQ+ people, making up roughly 22% of all reported hate crimes.[76] UCLA's

Williams Institute found that LGBTQ+ people experience a higher rate of serious crime, which is defined as rape, sexual assault, robbery, or aggravated assault than non-LGBTQ+ people "53.7 vs 8.5 per 1,00" and more broadly they "experienced 106.4 violent victimizations17 per 1,000 persons, and transgender people experienced victimization at a rate of 93.7 per 1,000, compared with 21.1 per 1,000 among non-LGBTq+ persons."[77]Alongside these heightened levels of violence, queer people, particularly transgender people, reported significant mental health concerns. The Trevor Project's 2024 US National Survey found that queer youth in the age range of 13–24 are at significantly higher rates of suicide risk than non-queer youth.[78] That risk is caused in part by heightened stigma directed toward queer people.

Importantly, studies reveal that respectability politics has not in fact changed cisgender heterosexuals' perspective on LGBTQ+ rights.[79] Arguments in support of mainstreaming do not reflect the claims frequently made in terms of assimilation - that LGBTQ+ people will be safer and more respected. The appeal, in ways, is that in becoming legible by the State through assimilation, that one will be able to fully participate in civic and political life. However, as previously mentioned, the legibility of queerness and queer bodies contributes to regulation and control, rather than freedom. Moreover, the further one is from the legible queer body—white, cisgender, wealthy—the more one body is regulated and constrained. Even though transgender people are protected by laws such as Title IX, their ability to use and access these rights is increasingly challenged. Trans bodies are, within this metric, always other and perpetually queer.

The History and Evolution of Criminalizing Gender Nonconformity

Transgender people demonstrate that gender is in fact mutable. The fears surrounding social transitioning demonstrate a fear not just of physical and bodily change, but also that the social fabric can make room for people to assert their gender identity, and to have that respected. Transgender women in particular experience specific hostilities related to their deviations from patriarchal norms, in which maleness is something to which one should aspire. Transgender women represent a rejection of manhood, and experience significant violence due to this perceived betrayal of cisgender heterosexual patriarchy.

Transgender women have often been mischaracterized as "men in dresses," exemplified by the infamous case of Mary Jones—the so-called "man-monster"—who was put on trial in 1836 for allegedly stealing a client's wallet.[80] The court and newspapers became captivated by Jones, who dressed as a woman and engaged in sexual relationships with men, using an artificial vagina crafted from cow leather.[81] In another well-known case, Lucy Hicks Anderson, a Black transgender woman and socialite in California, was prosecuted in 1945 for perjury and fraud after a court-ordered medical examination revealed she had been assigned male at birth. She received a ten-year probation sentence in lieu of imprisonment.[82] As a condition of her release, she was ordered to wear masculine clothing after the court deemed her a "man impersonating woman."[83]

In addition to weaponizing criminal codes for offenses such as theft, perjury, and fraud, most US states enforced anti-cross-dressing and anti-"masquerade" laws from the nineteenth century through much of the twentieth century. In fact, according to Kate Redburn, by the 1960s, nearly every city across the United States had anti-cross-dressing laws on the books.[84] Such laws criminalized any individual who "shall appear upon any public street or other public place... in a dress not belonging to his or her sex."[85] Some towns only criminalized cross-dressing "with intent to conceal his or her sex," while others only prohibited "cross-dressing with intent to commit a crime," as in San Diego.[86] In other cities, such as Detroit and Miami Beach, "ordinances specified only that men could not wear women's clothes in public."[87] According to Redburn, most of these measures were enacted under the municipal police power—a broad and often vaguely defined authority allowing cities to legislate for the "health, safety, morals, and welfare of their citizens."[88] These statutes disproportionately targeted transgender people, gender-nonconforming folks, and drag performers. As Clare Sears explains, cross-dressing laws served as a "central mechanism for policing a whole series of 'belongings', not only the items of clothing that 'belonged' to a specific sex but also the types of people that 'belonged' in public spaces and the types of bodies that 'belonged' in the categories of man and woman."[89] According to Sears, from the 1940s to the 1970s, hundreds of people were arrested under these laws each year in major cities.[90]

In New York City, the previously mentioned "three-article rule," was repeatedly enforced against Stonewall figures like Marsha P. Johnson and Sylvia Rivera and is often cited as a catalyst for the Stonewall Riots after police busted in to arrest patrons under this policy.[91] While these laws most often targeted transgender women and cross-dressing men, they were also enforced against drag kings and transgender men. For example, Stormé DeLarverie, a Black butch lesbian and drag king, was also arrested multiple times for wearing "male" clothing and was among those who resisted at Stonewall.[92]

By the 1970s, cross-dressing laws were fading, but other laws emerged to target the same communities.[93] Campbell has argued that laws like New York's Section 240.37 Loitering for the Purpose of Engaging in a Prostitution Offense, which was enacted in 1976, are extensions of cross-dressing laws that enabled the State to continually remind transgender and gender-nonconforming people that they do not belong in society.[94] According to Campbell, the New York Police Department (NYPD) used this law to justify targeting and profiling transgender women for wearing tight or "revealing" clothing.[95] Similarly to cross-dressing laws and other statutes used to regulate queer subjects, "These bans solidified the boundaries around who and what is acceptable, and in doing so, played a critical role in upholding the cis-heteronormative national identity."[96] The necropolitics of the State's regulation of queer bodies in order to uphold national identity were expressed in the response to the AIDS epidemic.

Queer as in Contamination

Laws regulating sexuality—aimed at preventing the so-called "contamination" of queer sexuality[97]—were perhaps most visible during the AIDS epidemic of the 1980s. During this decade, local, State, and federal governments expanded laws and policing practices that isolated and criminalized those most affected—sex workers, gay men, and transgender women.[98] Many states invoked or strengthened communicable disease statutes to permit forced testing, isolation, and quarantine of people suspected of having HIV/AIDS.[99] Over thirty states enacted HIV-specific criminal laws, punishing acts such as consensual sex, spitting, or biting—even without any risk of transmission.[100] At the federal level, a 1987 ban barred HIV-positive immigrants and visitors until 2010,[101] and the 1990 Ryan White CARE Act tied HIV/AIDS funding to State laws criminalizing knowing HIV exposure.[102]

In cities such as New York and San Francisco, moral policing laws—including anti-sodomy, lewd conduct, and public decency provisions[103]—were increasingly deployed under the guise of public health.[104] In 1985,

New York City officials ordered the closure of several gay bathhouses, including the St. Mark's Baths, citing "high-risk sexual activity,"[105] while San Francisco's Department of Public Health, with police cooperation, shut down nearly all commercial gay bathhouses.[106] Public parks and other known gay cruising areas saw intensified policing for alleged "public indecency,"[107] and HIV-positive sex workers were subjected to heightened surveillance and criminalization.[108]

Melinda Cooper notes that the AIDS epidemic was used as a way to reinforce conservatism and neoliberalism through the economics of healthcare. Private hospitals had the right to turn away the indigent, and the creation of Medicaid became a threat to profits. ACT UP, AIDS Coalition to Unleash Power, was a significant organizing group that focused on healthcare specifically. They argued specifically for universalized healthcare, one unconnected to wages or employment. Although ACT UP is frequently identified as wealthy and white, historical records reflect that nearly one third of men involved in meetings of one NYC chapter were largely uninsured.[109] The effort to organize so that HIV-positive people could access medical care through avenues such as Medicaid, raised debates over who is "worthy of care." Daniel Wikler argues that patients who develop an illness due to their own choices have a personal responsibility rather than a larger political or social responsibility.[110] The government has no obligation to individuals who are HIV-positive. HIV-positive people are responsible for their own care, and society has no obligations to care for those who make "poor choices." Cooper notes that the AIDS epidemic cynically became an argument for same-sex marriage due to spousal insurance. The HIV-positive person would no longer be cared for by the public, but by their spouse.[111] This conservative argument diverges significantly from ACT UP's demands for universalized healthcare. The responsibilization of healthcare within contemporary conservatism is inseparable from the responsibilization of neoliberalism.

Neoliberalism isolates individuals, and by posing all actions as done using a cost-benefit analysis, individuals may "win" or they may "lose" depending upon their choices. This ultimately contributes to individuals identified as "undeserving" due to their individual choices, rather than by an examination of larger social and political strictures which contribute to one's access to choices. Assimilationist politics allow for queer people to have *more* choices due to having more access to privilege. It is possible, then, for HIV-positive people to receive care through access to marriage.

Within an assimilationist framework, marginalized communities become accepted only by distancing themselves from those aspects of identity which are seen as obscene and disgusting, which in contemporary politics often results in the exclusion of transgender people from civic society.

Conclusion

The direct criminalization of the LGBTQ+ community, as well as more discrete forms of surveillance, is ultimately regulation of legibility. Hil Malatino writes, "To be made juridically illegible is a form of erasure and exclusion, to be sure, but it's not as if we'll stop actually existing on account of how we're interpellated by Health and Human Services."[112] Much as with other assaults on LGBTQ+ populations, people with disabilities, and individuals in need of reproductive care—these populations will continue to exist regardless of whether the law acknowledges them or not. However, when bodies are made *hyper-visible* by the law, in this specific case being transgender and gender-nonconforming people, those bodies are frequently established as an Other and are the site of disgust. The rejection of those Other bodies can act as a way to access power and privilege, to be made less hyper-visible.

February 2025, the National Park Service removed all mention of transgender people from their page on the Stonewall Uprising. The LGBTQ+ acronym is now "LGB" or "LGBQ." "Queer" is also not on the page. July 10, 2025, journalist Erin Reed brought to light that the webpage for Stonewall had removed "bisexuals" from the website as well.[113] The push to enforce gender normativity, and erase transgender people from civic life and history, does not inherently lead to the safety of other members of the LGBTQ+ community.[114] The removal of bisexuals from the history of Stonewall is illustrative of the dangers of accepting the exclusion of transgender and gender-nonconforming people in the pursuit of assimilation.

The assimilationist argument is grounded in a neoliberal and conservative framework, but ultimately returns to liberal contentions that it is through rights that people are guaranteed recognition and thereby protections by the State. However, even with the inclusion of transgender and gender-conforming into anti-discrimination laws, in particular Title IX, these communities are increasingly facing erasure from civic life, supported by public LGBTQ+ figures such as Buttigeig.

This erasure of transgender and gender nonconforming people illustrates a lack of interest in difference, and contributes to the direct turning away of the Other. Difference, much like vulnerability, is an essential aspect of being. Levinas' development of an ethical standard based upon how we treat the stranger is particularly salient in this regard. Transgender and gender-nonconforming are a minority population yet are hyper-visible and experience continuous attacks on their personhood. While transgender and gender-nonconforming people should not be thought of as strangers or outside of the larger civic and political community, and recent restrictions on research pertaining to transgender people makes gathering data on these communities especially difficult, many polls report that less than 3% of the total US population identify as transgender.[115] For many people, transgender people are strangers whom they are unlikely to meet in their daily lives. Yet, transgender people occupy a very public site of discourse around rights and dignity, unlike other members of the LGBTQ+ community. Thus, any laws pertaining to transgender and gender-nonconforming people ought to be approached with careful attentiveness so as not to contribute to language that further isolates these populations, singling them out as uniquely Other, when these communities have always been a part of civic and political life.

If we approach legal embodiment through this perspective, legibility does not need to entail discrimination and violence. Care, therefore, stands in direct opposition to the State's technologies, which embed normative ways of relating to one another and of performing the self within the body.[116] Instead of using State technologies to enforce such norms through disciplinary apparatuses that regulate and control certain bodies in order to, in Lucile Richard's words, "optimize political obedience and economic gain," the law can come from an understanding that we are all different vulnerable beings and are all in need of care.[117] This ideology shifts us from asking to be assimilated into the normative, unseen, and forgotten body, to encouraging difference.

Even as queer people's rights are being challenged, the percentage of individuals in the United States identifying as LGBTQ+ has increased from 4% in 2012 to 8% in 2023.[118] The ability for non-heterosexuals to live openly has significantly increased with assimilationist policies, which in turn contributes to people being more able to identify as non-heterosexual. Although we disagree with the philosophy behind these legal approaches, they have undoubtedly contributed positively for some members of the queer community. However, as some members of the community have gained acceptance, transgender people have been increasingly abandoned by other members of the LGBTQ+ community. The experience of being targeted by both the states and being abandoned by one's community is a lapse in political ethics. It is this lack to which we must attend.

We have responsibility toward others. Responsibilization, through the marriage of neoliberalism and social conservatism, is the antithesis to this form of collective responsibility. Responsibility is a form of attending to another's needs, a necessary category of care as outlined by Joan Tronto. To fully understand one's obligation to another requires some knowledge of them. We therefore are moved to learn about differences in order to provide accurate care. Care is not totalizing. It must be responsive to an individual and a community's needs. Legal embodiment grounded in this form of responsibility supports diverse forms of sexuality, gender, and gender expression. It does not seek to confine or to surveil, so much as to expand and to support.

Notes

1. Abby Monteil, "Pete Buttigieg Says Trans Athletes in Women's Spots Raise 'Serious Fairness Issues,'" *Them*, July 29, 2025.
2. Blair Hamilton, Andrew Brown, Stephanie Montagner-Moraes, Cristina Comeras-Chueca, Peter G. Bush, Fergus M. Guppy, and Yannis P. Pitsiladis, "Strength, Power and Aerobic Capacity of Transgender Athletes: A Cross-sectional Study," *British Journal of Sports Medicine* 58, no. 11 (2024): 586–597.
3. Aeyal Gross, "Gender Outlaws Before the Law: The Courts of the Borderlands," *Dukeminier Awards: Best Sexual Orientation & Gender Identity L. Rev.* 9(2010): 159.
4. Catherine A. Lugg, "Thinking About Sodomy: Public Schools, Legal Panopticons, and Queers," *Educational Policy*, no. 1 (2006), 39.
5. Eskridge Jr, William N. "Challenging the Apartheid of the Closet: Establishing Conditions for Lesbian and Gay Intimacy, Nomos, and Citizenship, 1961–1981." *Hofstra L. Rev.* 25 (1996): 817.
6. Hugh Ryan, "How Dressing in Drag Was Labeled a Crime in the 20th Century," *History.com*, June 25, 2019, https://www.history.com/articles/stonewall-riots-lgbtq-drag-three-article-rule.

7. Ethan Dunn, “Silencing and Surveillance: The Struggle of Same-Sex Desire in the Shadow of the 20thCentury Police State” (2024). Honors Theses. 669.
8. Catherine A. Lugg, “Thinking About Sodomy.”
9. Alan Hyde, 252.
10. Margot Canaday, *The Straight State.*
11. Janet E. Halley, “Reasoning about sodomy: Act and identity in and after Bowers v. Hardwick,” *Va. L. Rev.* 79 (1993): 1721.
12. Catherine A. Lugg, 40.
13. Maya Campbell, “Perceived to Be Deviant”: Social Norms, Social Change, and New York State’s ‘Walking While Trans’ Ban,” *Cal. L. Rev.* 110 (2022): 1065.
14. Dean Spade, *Normal Life*,73.
15. Ibid., 73–74.
16. Ibid., 74.
17. Max Osborn, “LGBTQIA+ Individuals’ Encounters with Police: Contextual Factors, Help-Seeking, and Service Needs,” ProQuest Dissertations & Theses, 2022, 36.
18. Tabitha Adams, “The Progression of the LGBTQ+ Rights Movement in the United States: The Human Rights Campaign,” (2019).
19. Catherine A. Lugg, “Thinking About Sodomy,” 39.
20. Dean Spade, “Documenting Gender,” Hastings Law Journal 59, no. 3 (2008): 731–842.
21. Urvashi Vaid, *Virtual Equality: The Mainstreaming of Gay and Lesbian Politics* (New York: Anchor Books, 1995) 3.
22. Gabriele Magni, “Nearly 240 Anti-LGBTQ Bills Filed in 2022 So Far, With Most Targeting Trans People.” *NBC News*, March 20, 2022; Anxieties over transgender people’s access to public spaces, such as bathrooms, build on more than a century of regulation targeting queer and gender-nonconforming people— people who were pathologized and confined to psychiatric or criminal institutions under the guise of preventing violence, deviance, and perversity. Rhetoric about “safety,” particularly the protection of white women and children, has historically been used to justify cross-dressing laws, as well as statutes criminalizing lewdness and vagrancy. See Kate Redburn, “Before Equal Protection: The Fall of Cross-Dressing Bans and the Transgender Legal Movement, 1963–86,” *40 Law and History Review* 679 (2022); William N. Eskridge Jr., “Law and the construction of the closet: American

regulation of same-sex intimacy, 1880–1946," *Iowa L. Rev.* 82 (1996): 1007.

23. Hannah Fingerhut, "Iowa's Civil-Rights Protections No Longer Include Gender Identity as New Law Takes Effect." *Associated Press*, July 1, 2025. https://apnews.com/article/iowa-civil-rights-code-gender-identity-d90d374e821b5663b8114eef27e8d03d.
24. Zane McNeill, "How the Trump Administration Is Undermining Civil Rights Law—and How Nonprofits Can Fight Back." *Nonprofit Quarterly*, April 14, 2025. https://nonprofitquarterly.org/how-the-trump-administration-is-undermining-civil-rights-law-and-how-nonprofits-can-fight-back/.
25. Williams Institute, "New Executive Order Removes Workplace Protections for More Than 114,000 Transgender Federal Employees and LGBTQ Employees of Federal Contractors," *Williams Institute*. https://williamsinstitute.law.ucla.edu/press/nd-protections-eo-press-release/.
26. Zane McNeill, "Denver Schools Face Federal Inquiry Over All-Gender Restroom." *Truthout*, January 29, 2025. https://truthout.org/articles/denver-schools-face-federal-inquiry-over-all-gender-restroom/.
27. Mulvihill, Geoff. "States Sue Trump, Saying He Is Intimidating Hospitals Over Gender-Affirming Care for Youth." *Associated Press*, August 1, 2025. https://apnews.com/article/trump-gender-affirming-care-lawsuit-hospitals-dfc156f4bffcf4b6136658207488d17d.
28. Zane McNeill, "USDA Suspends Maine Education Funds Over State's Support for Trans Athletes." *Truthout*, April 3, 2025. https://truthout.org/articles/usda-suspends-maine-education-funds-over-states-support-for-trans-athletes/.
29. T. Anansi Wilson,"Black, Trans(Gressive) Lives: Furtive Blackness & The Surround of Extralegal Violence." *Geo. J. Gender & L.* 26 (2024).
30. Ibid., 232.
31. Paige Osburn, "'No Justice, No Pride' Protest Highlights Fault Lines in D.C. LGBTQ Community," WAMU, June 11, 2017, accessed August 10, 2025, https://wamu.org/story/17/06/11/no-justice-no-pride-protest-highlights-fault-lines-d-c-lgbtq-community/.

32. Zane McNeill, and Kyra Smith. "Whose Pride Is This Anyway? The Quare Performance of the# Black Pride4." In *The Palgrave Handbook of Queer and Trans Feminisms in Contemporary Performance*, pp. 203–222. Cham: Springer International Publishing, 2021.
33. Greey, Ali. "Queer inclusion precludes (Black) queer disruption: Media analysis of the Black lives matter Toronto sit-in during Toronto Pride 2016." In *Leisure, Racism, and National Populist Politics*, pp. 15–29. Routledge, 2021; Khyree D. Davis, "Transnational Blackness at Toronto Pride: Queer Disruption as Theory and Method." *Gender, Place and Culture* 28, no. 11 (2021): 1541–1560.
34. Doualy Xaykaothao, "Protesters Briefly Halt Pride Parade," MPR News, June 25, 2017. https://www.mprnews.org/story/2017/06/25/protesters-briefly-halt-pride-parade.
35. Zane McNeill and Kyra Smith, Whose Pride Is This Anyway?".
36. Zane McNeill and Blu Buchanan. "Tracing the Color of Queer Choreopolitics." *The Activist History Review*, January 13, 2020, https://activisthistory.com/2020/01/13/tracing-the-color-of-queer-choreopolitics/; Marc Spindelman, "Symposium: Sexual Orientation, Gender Identity, & the Constitution: Queer Black Trans Politics and Constitutional Originalsim." *ConLawNOW* 13, no. 2 (2021): 5.
37. Zane McNeill, "From Courts to Community Power: Trans Rights Advocates Respond to Skrmetti's Fallout." *Nonprofit Quarterly*, August 4, 2025. https://nonprofitquarterly.org/from-courts-to-community-power-trans-rights-advocates-respond-to-skrmettis-fallout/.
38. "A Conversation About Skrmetti With Ezra Young & Naomi Schoenbaum." Assigned Media, July 8, 2025. https://www.assignedmedia.org/breaking-news/skrmetti-interview-ezra-young-naomi-schoenbaum.
39. Scott Skinner-Thompson, "Trans Animus". Boston College Law Review 65, no.3(2024): 965–1028.
40. Scott Skinner-Thompson, "The Faulty Logic behind the Supreme Court's Failure to Protect Trans Minors," *New England Journal of Medicine* 393 (2025): 316.
41. *Skrmetti* has already prompted expanding court decisions undermining equal protection, parental rights, and first amendment

protections. See *Brandt v. Rutledge*, No. 23–2681 (8th Cir. Aug. 12, 2025).
42. Scott Skinner-Thompson, "Transgender Disenfranchisement," *Washington University Law Review* 102 (2025), U of Colorado Law Legal Studies Research Paper No. 25-1 (January 17, 2025).
43. Anansi T. Wilson, "Black, Trans(Gressive) Lives."
44. While outside the scope of this book, much of these histories were also part of a continuing colonial project which sought to control and erase Indigenous gender systems. See Scott Lauria Morgensen, *Spaces Between Us: Queer Settler Colonialism and Indigenous Decolonization* (University of Minnesota Press, 2011) and Jeremiah A. Ho, "Colonizing Queerness." *U. Colo. L. Rev.* 95 (2024): 889.
45. *United States v. Skrmetti*, 145 S. Ct. 1816, 1881.
46. Alan Sears, "30 Years On: The Toronto Bathhouse Raids and Sexual and Gender Liberation," *Socialist Project*, February 26, 2011, https://socialistproject.ca/2011/02/b471/.
47. Matt Markovich, "Police Deny LGBTQ Bar Visits Were Raids; Officials Change Lewd Laws," *MyNorthwest*, January 31, 2024, https://mynorthwest.com/local/police-deny-lgbtq-bar-visits-raids-officials-change-lewd-laws/3948822.
48. Brianna Willis, "Dozens Arrested During Houston Police Department Raid at La Zona Bar & Lounge and Los Corrales South, Officials Say," ABC13 Houston, May 10, 2025, https://abc13.com/post/dozens-arrested-during-houston-police-depart ment-raid-la-zona-bar-lounge-los-corrales-south-officials-say/16376485/.
49. Ibid.
50. Zane McNeill, "From Courts to Community Power."
51. Zane McNeill, "Stacking the Courts against Mifepristone." *Political Research Associates*, February 12, 2025. https://politicalres earch.org/2025/02/12/stacking-courts-against-mifepristone.
52. Zane McNeill, "Want to Honor Trans Day of Visibility? Fight With Us Like Your Life Hinges on It." *Truthout*, March 31, 2025. https://truthout.org/articles/want-to-honor-trans-day-of-visibility-fight-with-us-like-your-life-hinges-on-it/.
53. Senthorun Raj, "Disturbing disgust: Gesturing to the abject in queer cases." In *Queering criminology*, pp. 83–101. (London: Palgrave Macmillan UK, 2016).

54. *Miller v. California*, 413 U.S. 15.
55. "Testimony for PA House of Representatives Judiciary Committee," Claudia Brenner, April 22, 1992 and August 28, 1995, https://www.legis.state.pa.us/WU01/LI/TR/Transcripts/1995_0089_0011_TSTMNY.pdf.
56. Senthorun Raj, "Disturbing Disgust."
57. Martha Nussbaum, *Hiding from Humanity*, 74.
58. Before the emergence of modern anti-sodomy laws, earlier regulatory schemes criminalized offenses such as "buggery," "lying with men," "carnal knowledge," and "crimes against nature."
59. Senthorun Raj, "Disturbing Disgust," 85.
60. Ibid, 83.
61. Michael E. Brewer, "Sodomy Laws and Privacy-The Cost of Keeping Gays in the Closet." *Denv. UL Rev.* 79 (2001): 546.
62. Ibid., 547.
63. Lawrence R. Matthew, "Defining the crime against nature: Sodomy in the United States appeals courts, 1810–1940." *Journal of Homosexuality* 19, no. 1 (1990): 49–66.
64. Michael E. Brewer, "Sodomy Laws and Privacy." This absence was not so much a sign of tolerance, but rather a patriarchal disregard for female sexuality—namely, when it lay outside male sight and regulation. Lesbianism was not as targeted as male homosexuality, and the gender performances and sexuality of trans women, were because it was not thought of as a threat to the male sexual identity or the reproductive imperative on which patriarchy rested. See Sidney Wegener, *The Emergence of Lesbianism from Women's Penal Institutions: Incarcerated Women-Loving Women, Interracial Coupling, and Women's Blues Music, 1895–1935* (master's thesis, Sarah Lawrence College, 2021) and Hugh Ryan, *The Women's House of Detention: A Queer History of a Forgotten Prison* (New York: Bold Type Books, 2022).
65. Michael E. Brewer, "Sodomy Laws and Privacy," 546, 547.
66. Hugh Ryan, "Who's Afraid of Social Contagion?" *Boston Review*, July 31, 2023. https://www.bostonreview.net/articles/whos-afraid-of-social-contagion/; William Eskridge Jr., "Law and the Construction of the Closet."
67. Michael E. Brewer, "Sodomy Laws and Privacy," 546, 547.
68. Death Penalty Information Center, "Criminalization of Homosexuality in American History," last modified September 25,

2024, https://deathpenaltyinfo.org/policy-issues/biases-and-vulnerabilities/lgbtq-people/criminalization-of-homosexuality-in-american-history.

69. Judith Adkins, "These People Are Frightened to Death: Congressional Investigations and the Lavender Scare." *Prologue* 48, no. 2 (Summer 2016): 6–20. https://www.archives.gov/publications/prologue/2016/summer/lavender.html.
70. William N. Eskridge Jr., *Dishonorable Passions: Sodomy Laws in America, 1861–2003* (New York: Viking, 2008).
71. Janet E. Halley, "Reasoning about sodomy," 1721, 1729.
72. Ryan Goodman, "Beyond the enforcement principle: Sodomy laws, social norms, and social panoptics." *Calif. L. Rev.* 89 (2001): 643.
73. *Lawrence v. Texas*, 539 U.S. 558 (2003).
74. Martha Nussbaum, *Hiding from Humanity,* 113.
75. Kalysha Closson, Sabrina C. Boyce, Nicole Johns, David J. Inwards-Breland, Edwin Elizabeth Thomas, and Anita Raj. "Physical, sexual, and intimate partner violence."
76. "FBI Releases 2022 Crime in the Nation Statistics."
77. "Anti-LGBT Victiminization in the United States," *The Williams Institute.*
78. "2024 U.S. National Survey on the Mental Health of LGBTQ+ Young People," *The Trevor Project.*
79. Philip Edward Jones, "Respectability politics and straight support for LGB rights.“ *Political Research Quarterly* 75, no. 4 (2022): 935–949.
80. C. Riley Snorton, *Black on Both Sides: A Racial History of Trans Identity* (Minneapolis: University of Minnesota Press, 2017), 60.
81. Jonathan Katz, "Love stories: Sex between men before homosexuality.“ *(No Title)* (2001).
82. "Lucy Hicks Anderson," *Legacy Project Chicago.* https://legacyprojectchicago.org/person/lucy-hicks-anderson.
83. Shari Rose, "Lucy Hicks Anderson: Black Transgender Pioneer of the 1940s," Blurred Bylines, February 21, 2022. https://blurredbylines.com/articles/lucy-hicks-anderson-black-transgender-woman/.
84. Kate Redburn, "Before equal protection."
85. *Columbus v. Rogers*, 324 N.E.2d 563 (Ohio 1975).

86. *City of Chicago v. Wilson*, 389 N.E. 2d 522 (Ill. 1978); *City of Cincinnati v. Adams*, 330 N.E. 2d 463 (Ohio Municipal Court 1974).
87. "Court Voids Miami Beach Drag Ban"; "To Cross-Dressers Everywhere," Drag 2.7 (1972), 4; "San Diego Court Ruling Backs Clothing Ordinance," Drag 5.18, 1975, 5.
88. Ibid.
89. Clare Sears, *Arresting Dress: Cross-Dressing, Law, and Fascination in Nineteenth-Century San Francisco* (Durham: Duke University Press, 2015), 6.
90. Clare Sears, "This Isn't the First Time Conservatives Have Banned Cross-Dressing in America." Jacobin, March 15, 2023. https://jacobin.com/2023/03/cross-dressing-law-united-states-history-drag-bans.
91. Brett Wilkins, "Trump Administration Scrubs Transgender, Queer People From Stonewall Monument Website," *Common Dreams*, February 14, 2025. https://www.commondreams.org/news/stonewall-transgender.
92. Cal Goodin, "The Unsung Heroines of Stonewall," *National Parks Conservation Association* (blog), March 27, 2025. https://www.npca.org/articles/2736-the-unsung-heroines-of-stonewall.
93. While laws targeting prostitution expanded in the 1970s to encompass more queer and trans people, such laws had long been used against queer communities. As William N. Eskridge notes—and as seen in the cases of transgender and queer sex workers who were targeted and prosecuted—sex work regulations were frequently enforced against them, and, in turn, such "regulations were also readily applied or adapted to target same sex intimacy."
94. Maya Campbell, "Perceived to Be Deviant": Social Norms, Social Change, and New York State's" Walking While Trans" Ban." *Cal. L. Rev.* 110 (2022): 1065.
95. Ibid 1081.
96. Ibid 1088.
97. For more on AIDS, toxicity, and necropolitics, see Chen, Mel Y. "Toxic Animacies, Inanimate Affections." *GLQ* 17, no. 2–3 (2011): 265–86. doi:10.1215/10642684-1163400.
98. Jennifer Brier, *Infectious Ideas: U.S. Political Responses to the AIDS Crisis.* (Chapel Hill: University of North Carolina Press, 2009); James B. MacArthur, "As the tide turns: the changing

HIV/AIDS epidemic and the criminalization of HIV exposure." *Cornell L. Rev.* 94 (2008): 707.

99. Scott Burris, "Testing, Disclosure, and the Right to Privacy." In *AIDS Law Today: A New Guide for the Public*, edited by Scott Burris, Harlon L. Dalton, Judith Leonie Miller, and Yale AIDS Law Project, 115–49. Yale University Press, 1993.
100. Trevor Hoppe, *Punishing Disease: HIV and the Criminalization of Sickness* (Berkeley: University of California Press, 2018).
101. U.S. Department of Health and Human Services, "A Timeline of HIV and AIDS," HIV.gov, accessed August 9, 2025, https://www.hiv.gov/hiv-basics/overview/history/hiv-and-aids-timeline#year-1987.
102. Evelyn Mangold. "The Viral Injustice of HIV Criminalization." *The Regulatory Review*, February 24, 2022, https://www.theregreview.org/2022/02/24/mangold-viral-injustice-hiv-criminalization/.
103. Although such regulations had existed since the late nineteenth century to control queer sexuality, police increasingly used them to target gay cruising areas and bathhouses. See Law and the Construction of the Closet: American Regulation of Same-Sex Intimacy, 1880–1946, 82 Iowa L. Rev. 1007, 1033; William N. Eskridge Jr., Dishonorable Passions: Sodomy Laws in America, 1861–2003 (New York: Viking, 2008); Nan D. Hunter, "Life After Hardwick," Virginia Law Review 73, no. 6 (September 1987): 1205–1278.
104. Judith Rabin, Rabin, Judith A. "The AIDS epidemic and gay bathhouses: a constitutional analysis." *Journal of health politics, policy and law* 10, no. 4 (1986): 729–747; Scott Burris, "Legal aspects of regulating bathhouses: cases from 1984 to 1995." In *Gay Bathhouses and Public Health Policy*, pp. 131–151 (Routledge, 2013).
105. *City of New York v. New St. Mark's Baths*, 130 Misc. 2d 911, 497 N.Y.S. 2d 979 (N.Y. Sup. Ct. Jan. 6, 1986).
106. San Francisco AIDS Foundation. "Decades after San Francisco Closed Its Gay Bathhouses, a New Law Paves the Way for Their Return." *San Francisco AIDS Foundation,* February 12, 2020. https://www.sfaf.org/collections/breaking-news/decades-after-san-francisco-closed-its-gay-bathhouses-a-new-law-paves-the-way-for-their-return/.

107. William N. Eskridge Jr., "Challenging the Apartheid of the Closet."; Scott De Orio, "Bad queers: LGBTQ people and the Carceral State in modern America." *Law & Social Inquiry* 47, no. 2 (2022): 691–711.
108. Sienna Baskin, Aziza Ahmed, and Anna Forbes, "Criminal Laws on Sex Work and HIV Transmission: Mapping the Laws, considering the Consequences," *Denver Law Review* 93(2015); Arlene Zarembka & Katherine M. Franke, "Women in the AIDS Epidemic: A Portrait of Unmet Needs," *LOUIS. PUB. L. REV.* 9(1990): 519.
109. Melinda Cooper, *Family Values,* 207.
110. Daniel Wikler, "Persuasion and coercion for Health." *Paternalism* 37 (1983): 42–43; Daniel Wikler, "Who should be blamed for being sick?" *Health education quarterly* 14, no. 1 (1987): 11–25.
111. Melinda Cooper, 214.
112. Hil Malatino, *Trans* Care (Minneapolis: University of Minnesota Press, 2020), 11.
113. Erin Reed, "After Trans People, Trump Now Erasing Bisexual People from Stonewall National Monument," *Erin in the Morning,* July 10, 2025, https://www.erininthemorning.com/p/after-trans-people-trump-now-erasing.
114. Juliana Kim, "Park Service Erases 'Transgender' on Stonewall Website, Uses the Term 'GB' Movement," *National Public* Radio, February 14, 2025, https://www.npr.org/2025/02/14/g-s1-48923/stonewall-monument-transgender-park-service..
115. "LGBT + Pride 2023," *Ipsos,* https://www.ipsos.com/sites/default/files/ct/news/documents/2023-05/Ipsos%20LGBT%2B%20Pride%202023%20Global%20Survey%20Report%20-%20rev.pdf; "How Many Adults and Youth Identify as Transgender in the United States?" *Williams Institute,* https://williamsinstitute.law.ucla.edu/publications/trans-adults-united-states/.
116. Tina Vaittinen, "An Ethics of Needs."
117. Lucile Richard, "Pastoral Power, Sovereign Carelessness, and the Social Divisions of Care Work or: What Foucault Can Teach Us about the" Crisis of Care, *Foucault Studies* 36, no. 1 (2024): 331.
118. Lindsey Dawson, Jennifer Kates, Alex Montero, and Ashley Kirzinger, "LGBTQ+ Health Policy," *KFF*, September 30, 2024, https://www.kff.org/health-policy-101-lgbtq-health-policy/?entry=table-of-contents-introduction.

CHAPTER 6

Epilogue: The Body and the Sacred

Abstract We conclude the book with an epilogue that will act as a call to action. In this section we will propose an alternative approach to legal embodiment and the law. It is in this section that we will propose a care-based and intersectional model of approaching the law. We will address the need to develop a legal framework that foregrounds vulnerability theory and deprioritizes the liberal legal approach. The most recent anti-trans policies from the Trump administration have followed in the footsteps of the 1950s' Lavender Scare, when queer individuals had been demonized as threats to the social order and purged from the public sphere. As in the Lavender Scare, the contemporary attacks institutionalize cultural and legal anxieties to govern bodies and silence lives, constructing transgender people as threats to morality and public order. These policies are shocking revivals of State-sponsored discipline: they recall McCarthyism and its practices of surveillance and control targeted toward anyone perceived as deviant. By arguing for a rejection of these cycles of punishment through the anchoring of legal approaches in vulnerability theory, this epilogue envisions a legal system centered on care and protection that dismantles recurring scapegoating of marginalized groups and builds a more just and inclusive society.

Keywords Vulnerability · Care · Legal embodiment · Lavender Scare · McCarthyism

R. C. Valentine and Z. McNeill, *The Coercive Power of the Law*, https://doi.org/10.1007/978-3-032-07589-5_6

The body as property, the body as human need, the body as integrity—are all social constructions that create the very foundation they invoke. None rests on bodily experience, or at least, nothing in our experiences of our bodies leads necessarily either to Lockean property or communism or abortion rights.[1]

By virtue of their location within power, our bodies are also effective sites of resistance to power's capillary alignments... Since law is an effect of a stasis of power-relations, the structural co-implication of power and the body in the securing of legal obligation and obedience is the source for persistent and hopefully thorough-going legal transformation.[2]

Over the course of writing this book, the legal landscape of the United States has changed rapidly. Abortion access has largely been overturned. Gender-affirming healthcare bans and transphobic legislation has gained ground nationally, creating a new Lavender Scare. All these changes have rightfully sparked outrage and shock. Yet, for many people, these overturned rights had never been within their grasp. We have discussed how BBIPOC communities already experienced a two-tier citizenship regarding abortion access and reproductive healthcare.[3] Likewise, people with disabilities have had their lives managed and governed in strict ways. Solidarity and learning from these shared struggles, the overlaps and the differing ways in which bodies are surveilled, managed, and legislated provides us with a glimpse of possibilities for other political imaginations.

Our introduction ended with Simone Weil, and we would like to begin with that same passage:

> at the bottom of the heart of every human being, from earliest infancy until the tomb, there is something that goes on indomitably expecting, in the teeth all experience of crimes committed, suffered, and witnessed, that good and not evil will be done to him. It is this above all that is sacred in every human being...a political party busily seeking, or maintaining itself in power can discern nothing in these cries except a noise...it can never be capable of the tender and sensitive attention which is needed to understand its meaning.[4]

Weil wrote this essay, titled "Human Personality," in 1943, the same year of her death in England. 1943 was a critical year for European fascism. The Soviets won the Battle of Stalingrad against the Nazis, leading to the expulsion of the Nazis from the Soviet Union. Italy was invaded, and Mussolini was deposed and arrested. Yet, in this same year, Weil provided a scathing critique of liberalism in "Human Personality." Weil begins the essay by asking why don't we pluck the eyes out of a man walking by—is it the color of his hair or his eyes; is it his clothing? What is it about this *person* that prevents us from arbitrarily doing harm to him? It is not, in the end, these separate parts of him that make up his personality. No, for Weil it is our innate confidence in the care and concern of others, despite all the evidence to the contrary. Even as the Trump administration abuses and dehumanizes people, there is still a glimmering of hope that we see in how people continue about their days, caring for one another and living lives in spite of legal violence. Weil writes that when we cry out from harm, the State cannot hear our humanity in these cries, while the State is made up of people, because it is ultimately a system of power that relies upon the maintenance of power.

This calls for a reframing of the categories of being we have examined. For example, disability as a tool of governance is deeply embedded in the creation of inequality and exclusion. The ways disability is defined and managed must be questioned—not as neutral or protective measures, but as mechanisms of control that prioritize economic productivity and societal order over the dignity, autonomy, and lives of those labeled as deviant. When viewed through the lenses of biopolitics and necropolitics, disability reveals itself as more than a condition—it becomes a site of profound resistance. It is here, in the contestation of power over bodies and identities, that we can challenge oppressive systems and imagine new pathways toward justice and equality. It is not our discrete bodies that protect us from harm, in fact as we have examined, our vulnerable bodies cannot protect us from biopower. We ought not to expect the State to see our bodies as beautiful vulnerable things to protect, but we can demand that. If, as Eli Clare suggests, the body can be a site of resistance and, as we have explored in this book, the law is embodied within us—can we reimagine our relations through the lens of embodiment, as more than a disciplinary tool regulating our interactions with one another? If that is possible, what would that look like?[5]

What Weil describes as sacred, this hope in others in spite of all the evidence contrary to this hope, is a critical tool. In the moments when Riley needed physical aid due to a seizure in public, they have rarely awoken alone. Most times, there is a stranger there, rarely medically trained. This stranger was, for some reason, compelled to assist a stranger seizing. These moments of spontaneous care are what we return to when thinking of care. When Jonathan Herring writes that you can have a society without justice, but not a society without care—it is the stranger coming to the aid of a stranger that we think of. Care is not a vague directive. It is a material political ethic with material demands.

Care ethics emerged from feminist theory, and Carol Gilligan first used it to examine how young girls understand the world around them and their relationship to it and one another. Those girls related to one another by thinking of themselves as interconnected and interdependent. They were interested in how they embodied their morality.[6] We have sought to illustrate how legal embodiment functions and have critiqued it through the embodied morality of care ethics. The law is a tool, and it ought to be conceived of as such. The law is never neutral, and there is no stopping it from being used as a tool for care or as a tool of domination.

Caring Possibilities, Caring Difficulties

The utilization of the law as a tool for care requires that the law act to enforce and reify the tenets of care—responsibility, compassion, needs meeting, and attentiveness. To envision the law as a tool for care is difficult in a moment in which the State is deliberately wielding the law as a way to penalize marginalized minorities. Yet, the law can also act as a way to facilitate meeting needs. The Supreme Court, as of this writing, is poised to hear a case regarding the ADA in *A.J.T v. Osseo Area Schools*. The case is being brought by the parents of a Minnesota teenager, known as Ava in court papers. Ava has severe epilepsy and seizes in the morning. Her parents have sought unsuccessfully for her to have accommodations so that she can have a full school day beginning at noon. The Eighth Circuit and four other circuit courts follow a standard in which the student must prove a school district acts with bad faith or gross misjudgment. Lawyers for Ava point that neither the ADA nor the accompanying Section 504 of the Rehabilitation Act require "bad faith" or "gross misjudgment," and other individuals who sue, using these statutes outside of education do not need to meet those standards.[7] If the Supreme Court rules in favor of Ava, then people with disabilities would not need to meet higher standards to prove discrimination or to have meaningful access to education. This would be significant for people with disabilities, who make up 15% of national public school enrolling as of the 2021–2022 school year.[8] This ruling would not suddenly upend ableism within the United States, nor would it erase systemic boundaries people with disabilities continue to face; however, it would significantly benefit students with disabilities.

Even as there is a possible step forward for people with disabilities, the Trump Administration has been quick to attack people with disabilities.[9] After a deadly plane crash at the Ronald Reagan Washington National Airport, President Trump released a statement in which he blamed the Biden Administration's DEI policies, "Almost unbelievably, as a diversity, equity, and inclusion (DEI) initiative, the Biden FAA specifically recruited and hired individuals with 'severe intellectual' disabilities, psychiatric issues, and complete paralysis over other individuals who sought to work for the FAA."[10] In response to Trump, the National Disability Rights Network, the American Association of People with Disabilities, American Council of the Blind, Autistic Self Advocacy Network, Disability Rights Education and Defense Fund, United Spinal Association, National Federation of the Blind released the following statement:

> The President's remarks today suggesting the deadly crash of Flight 5342 may have been the fault of public servants with disabilities are irresponsible, disparaging, and wrong. It is extremely inappropriate for the President to use this tragedy as an opportunity to advance his anti-diversity hiring agenda. The focus of the federal government and the entire nation should be on the emergency response, a thorough investigation, and most of all, supporting the families and communities who lost their loved ones in this tragedy.
>
> People with disabilities proudly serve our nation through government service in every federal department and agency. Disabled employees, like non-disabled employees, are hired because they meet the qualifications needed to do the job. The Federal Aviation Administration has rigorous standards for hiring Air Traffic Controllers and all other FAA employees. Diversity hiring initiatives seek to expand the pool of potential qualified talent for a role – they do not supersede the qualifications and skills that the role requires. The implication that people are being hired to do a job for which they are unqualified is an unfounded lie that further reinforces harmful stereotypes against disabled people.[11]

People with disabilities exist in all spheres of life and have differing capacities. Trump illustrates a leadership style in which the disenfranchised and vulnerable are consistent targets and at risk of further disenfranchisement.[12]

The Trump administration has not shown itself to be particularly caring toward people with disabilities, and it has been hostile toward transgender people, creating a new lavender scare. Government websites in January 2025 erased pronouns from signatures and wiped public health information pertaining to transgender people from government websites.[13] Passports with the gender marker "X" are no longer allowed to be processed and created. Trump announced that he would pursue the banning of Medicaid funding gender-affirming care.[14] In the executive order "Defending Women from Gender Ideology Extremism and Restoring Biological Truth to the Federal Government" the administration asserts that being transgender infringes on women's rights and safety, despite a lack of evidence for this claim. The order connects transgender identities to the erosion of the American political system as well as truth, "The erasure of sex in language and policy has a corrosive impact not just on women but on the validity of the entire American system. Basing Federal policy on truth is critical to scientific inquiry, public safety, morale, and trust in government itself."[15] Nine days later on January 29, 2025, Trump released an executive order pertaining to education titled "Ending Radical Indoctrination in K-12 Schooling." This executive order refers to "gender ideology" as part of "anti-American ideologies" The order blocks educators from using a student's name and pronouns that align with their gender identity, and connects educators' support of transgender students to violations of civil rights, "Imprinting anti-American, subversive, harmful, and false ideologies on our Nation's children not only violates longstanding anti-discrimination civil rights law in many cases, but usurps basic parental authority."[16] This order blocks federal funding to schools which support students in social transitioning, or using curriculum that discusses gender as flexible or addresses systematic racism.[17]

These executive orders as well as the proliferation of anti-transgender bills are being challenged by courts as unconstitutional and a violation of civil rights. The ACLU is, as of this writing, challenging the Montana law, HB 121, which bars transgender and intersex people from "using restrooms and other sex-separated facilities that correspond to their gender identity in public spaces."[18] GLAD Law is filing lawsuits on behalf of transgender people in the military, challenging sections of an executive order requiring the Bureau of Prisons to house transgender women in men's prisons and withholding gender-affirming care, bans on nonbinary markers on passports, along with other court cases pertaining to transgender people's rights to participate in daily life and to be acknowledged in grants and policy.[19] These lawsuits are critical measures to fight against the dehumanization and eradication of transgender people from public life. Nonetheless, they cannot address what has allowed transphobic rhetoric and legislation to proliferate—transphobia itself.

Even with the hopeful possibilities of *A.J.T v. Osseo Area Schools* and the legal challenges against Trump's transphobic executive orders, a caring future requires not just court cases that promote people with disabilities and transgender peoples' rights, but a reorientation. We believe that reorientation is the social model of care. Akin to the social model in disability, which examines the disabling effects of society, the social model of care attends to society as care enabling. Court cases which extend and enshrine protections for people with disabilities, in this case, are care enabling. However, Trump's statements impede care. If we want to envision a caring future, it is first important to think through what a social model of care is.

The Social Model of Care

Care is both a disposition *and* an action. For a society to be caring citizens in their daily lives and the State through law must act in ways that are caring, but both citizens and the State must also be *disposed to care*. It is this latter facet that is the basis for the social model of care. To be disposed toward something or another necessitates that a person or a State must be inclined to do so. This requires the active cultivation of curiosity to difference.

Difference is any deviation from the normative liberal subject. Ultimately, all people exist as different due to our variations in abilities over our lifetime and our accompanying needs. We have looked at the law's attempts to render queer people and people with disabilities invisible, while also legally rendering them hyper-visible. The law renders certain bodies legible which may not otherwise be legible. This legibility does not necessarily need to be violent or discriminatory. If that legibility emerges from a dialogue between the law and those whom it is speaking about, then that legibility may come from a respect *for* difference, rather than an attempt to confine or constrain difference. The law must then express a caring curiosity, caring because it is based in the interest in understanding the Other, and the knowledge that we ourselves are also Others.

Curiosity is not value-neutral, and we ought not to pretend otherwise. What differentiates a curiosity based in disgust and one based on care is what is the hoped for outcome. Disgust demands that the object be hidden away, removed from society at large. It calls for discrimination. Care-based curiosity encourages connections. It looks for similarities in difference and delights in the divergences, rather than searching for ways to collapse all differences into a singular identity. If the State expresses this form of care, then we ought to see expansions in libraries, rather than limitations and funding cuts. Likewise, we would not see bans of gender-affirming care, nor would we see predetermined outcomes for pregnancies. Rather, we would see a State in which choice is prioritized.

Choice is frequently mistaken in terms of access. Our choices are always constrained in some way, simply by virtue of our lives. However, our choices may also be constrained due to access. If one simply cannot afford an abortion, or the travel necessary, then one will be pregnant and most likely give birth. Access often creates hierarchies of citizenship, in which those with the most access experience all the rights afforded to them. A caring society would not limit someone's choices or possible futures due to inaccessibility. A caring society would have a responsibility to ensure equal access. The social model of care necessitates a standard of living in which citizens and non-citizens alike have equal access to choices and opportunities. President Lyndon B. Johnson's War on Poverty originated from his belief that poverty was a symptom of greater social inequities:

> Very often a lack of jobs and money is not the cause of poverty, but the symptom. The cause may lie deeper in our failure to give our fellow citizens a fair chance to develop their own capacities... Let me make one principle of this administration abundantly clear: All of these increased opportunities -- in employment, in education, in housing, and in every field-must be open to Americans of every color. As far as the writ of Federal law will run, we must abolish not some, but all racial discrimination. For this is not merely an economic issue, or a social, political, or international issue. It is a moral issue, and it must be met by the passage this session of the bill now pending in the House.[20]

Johnson's words are as important now as they were in the 1960s. He speaks to poverty as interconnected to racial discrimination. If the State is caring, it has an obligation to investigate and to interrogate poverty and lack of opportunity's intersections with other forms of oppression. The State that is curious to difference and to whether that difference results in greater harm and exclusion, is a State that is obligated to act on those harms and to redress them.

Our curiosity to difference cultivates a disposition toward Others, and to recognizing our own Other-qualities. It is not the final end for the social model of care. The social model of care necessitates an embracing of responsibility as well as curiosity in difference.

Responsibility, as we define it, is an obligation toward others, whom we may or may not know. It is a duty which must be fulfilled, and if unfulfilled, results in some feeling of having done wrong. We may, over time, grow hardened by the pain of turning away from others; however, a carefully cultivated conscience necessitates an openness to feeling for others. Adam Smith defined this capacity as "sympathy," and he believed it was innate to all people:

> How selfish soever man may be supposed, there are evidently some principles in his nature, which interest him in the fortune of others, and render their happiness necessary to him, though he derives nothing from it, except the pleasure of seeing it. Of this kind is pity or compassion, the emotion which we feel for the misery of others, when we either see it, or are made to conceive it in a very lively manner. That we often derive sorrow from the sorrow of others, is a matter of fact too obvious to require any instances to prove it; for this sentiment, like all the other original passions of human nature, is by no means confined to the virtuous and humane, though they perhaps may feel it with the most exquisite sensibility. The greatest ruffian, the most hardened violator of the laws of society, is not altogether without it.[21]

Responsibility toward one another is grounded in this sense of sympathy. If I know that by turning away from my neighbor, I am causing him distinct distress, it will be difficult to do so. For this reason, I may distance myself from my neighbor, to prevent that distress, or our relationship may deepen. We can quickly move toward a society of siloed off individuals, hiding from the emotional repercussions of responsibility. Or we can use repercussions as guides for moral and ethical action. The social model of care necessitates a conscience informed and guided by sympathy, for what Smith eloquently describes in his *Theory of Moral Sentiments* as sympathy, may also be described as care.

When we examine recent legal challenges to the human dignity of marginalized populations, we see a lack of curiosity based in care. Rather, we see a curiosity based in discrimination, which erases queer people from public life even while vilifying them. Additionally, restrictions on abortion care necessarily impact those whose choices are restricted. The revival of the lavender scare illustrates a conception of politics and society in which we lack responsibility to all but ourselves. We, in all the smallness of that world, limit our imaginations of politics and the law if we look solely to our own experiences. The richness of future possibilities emerges solely from collaboration. The law is such one method of collaboration.

Caring Futures as Queer Futures as Crip Futures

Liberalism is a theory of individuals with our individual rights and our individual beings. Collaboration brings us together, and solidarity necessitates some level of community and identification with another person or group of persons. What ought we to organize around? Simone Weil leads us away from organizing around our individual separate identities, but to investigate some deeper shared quality. This is not to minimize organizing or actions around marginalized identities, particularly as marginalized groups are actively being persecuted. It is to claim however, that for broad solidarity-based movements, it is essential to find shared characteristics which bind us together. For Weil, it was the sacred. For us it is embodied difference.

As we have looked at the impacts of legal embodiment regarding limitations of reproductive and gender-affirming healthcare as well as the oppression of people with disabilities and queer people, the consistent thread throughout is the usage of the law to dehumanize. Any movement to combat this must return to embodied difference. Our differences, particularly in this case in terms of legal embodiment, illustrate a need for a politics of a commitment to mutual liberation despite *and* because of difference. When Eli Clare speaks of embracing crip bodies, including the things we may want to avoid in our discussion of disability, we can also see this in the discussion of queer visibility, and how queer people ought to represent themselves so as to be accepted by cisgender heterosexual people. Within these experiences, our difference is made hyper-visible to ourselves and others. Visibility itself is not always comfortable, but it can be a tool for organizing around principles of mutual liberation.

The disability framework encompasses all people, as we will all be disabled throughout our lives. Similarly, queer frameworks give a voice for individuals whose lives and experiences diverge from what is understood as normative.[22] The social model of care framework seeks to embrace these frameworks, in which the voices of the vulnerable are the voices of the powerful. Joan Tronto described care ethics as a form of ethics in which the powerful are the vulnerable. By placing power in the hands of the vulnerable, who most clearly utilize, in some form or fashion, networks of care, we move away from a liberal construct of the autonomous self-interested rational individual. The powerful person in a liberal framework is the one who needs the *least*. Whereas in the social model of care, we begin from the premise that all people are needy. This neediness is a positive quality that binds us together, rather than separating us.

Legalizing Caring

The role of the State in realizing care is significant. Liberal thinkers have grappled with how the State ought to participate in this realization. Nussbaum and Sen's breakthrough with their capabilities approach was to imagine what aspects of life are necessary for a complete life, yet even within this, vulnerability is identified as a burden, "Any real society is a caregiving and care-receiving society, and must therefore discover ways of coping with these facts of human neediness and dependency that are compatible with the self-respect of the recipients and do not exploit caregivers."[23] This is certainly an improvement on traditional liberalism; however, posing human needs as something that society must *cope* with, contributes to a conception of vulnerability which is ultimately negative. If society copes with Riley's epilepsy and needs rather than sees their unique needs and experiences as something to be uplifted, the stigma against people with epilepsy and other disabilities as a burden is in some way justified. We do not want to live in a world in which ableism is condoned or built into our conception of what it means to live a good life. Rather, we want to live in a world in which difference, including difference of ability, is seen as something to be celebrated.

Although we have extended the discussion of care and the law beyond medical care, that is where we most frequently encounter debates over care. Indeed, Nussbaum and other liberals focus largely on disability in their consideration of need and care. The major question behind medical law and care is who owns our bodies? Is it us? The State? Our families? The ownership of our bodies evolves over time. Our immediate guardians are the first safe guarders of our bodies. Yet, even within this, children and adolescents are granted some rights over their bodies. When a child is abused, it is their human being which is violated, and not that of their guardians. The debate over bodily ownership is bound up with conceptions of personhood. It is for that reason, debates over late-term abortions as opposed to early-term abortions, frequently return to questions of whether or not the fetus is a person and thereby afforded some level of protections.

The question of who owns my body is not easily separable. If we are recognized as persons before the law, then we are all granted some level of ownership over our bodies. Yet, for the liberal nonpersons, they do not own their bodies. Even so, we often pause at decisions over whether or not to "pull the plug" on life support. It is difficult to look at someone who is utterly dependent on life support and view them as a nonperson. Even in this position, they are still afforded human dignity. It is illegal to abuse the body of a person, regardless of whether they are conscious or not. Indeed, it is illegal to mutilate and harm the corpse of a dead person. In some ways, we view the body as something that deserves respect, and the violation of the body invokes disgust. It is not our task to determine where this disgust comes from, but it is revelatory. Bodies, particularly vulnerable bodies, are seen as worthy of protection.

Our bodies are constantly interacting with the world around us, from birth to death we are always responding to the world.[24] The openness of our bodies is something which we cannot control. As two transgender nonbinary people, this openness can be nerve wracking. Trans people are often at risk precisely due to their bodies not meeting normative standards for what a body *ought* to look like. Being trans can often result in feeling as though our bodies are not ours, as they are forcibly interpreted by the world; perhaps reinterpreted when we assert our own understanding of ourselves, but the openness to the world can at times feel more akin to an open wound than to a welcome experience. A caring approach to the law must recognize that different bodies experience the world differently and may need protection from the world. Openness is something we have praised, particularly regarding curiosity, but it is undeniable that openness also carries with it risk of violence. The law must be flexible in its approach, and recognize that different bodies come with different needs, which ought to be respected. In contrast to the biopolitical legal order—which controls bodies through disciplinary and lethal apparatuses that render those deemed without political value both killable and disposable—care demands that vulnerable populations be recognized as more than merely controllable, coerced, surveilled, extracted from, exploited, or killed.[25] If, as Lee Edelman posits, the State is predicated on a reproductive futurism centered on "the child"—an imagined white, cisgender, heterosexual figure on which the future itself is built—then this demands a legal reimagining of whose lives are deemed worthwhile to the State and, in tandem, what futures we would like to build beyond the limitations of a judicial system founded on controlling the bodies and relations of the subject.[26] This requires a complete reconsideration of the relationship between bodies and the law.[27]

Theory or Praxis?

There is ultimately within all political theory, a tension between theory and praxis. Theory is necessary, yet it runs the risk of devouring any and all possible action underneath the weight of debate. Praxis without the reflective process of critique holds the possibility of acting without understanding *why* one is doing so and in doing so leading to a vapid politics. We have hoped to walk a line between the two. Bernard Harcourt argues that liberalism is ultimately built on illusions, as are all political theories. Harcourt contends liberalism's illusions are that the law is neutral; this neutralization of the law facilitates an acceptance of the outcomes of the law as inevitable and natural. Yet, the law is constructed by people, and as Harcourt writes, "we are *our* actions. We are *our* political decisions."[28] Harcourt argues we get to decide how our world runs and the truths upon which it operates. While we may pause at the idea that *all* things are constructed in some way and there are no truths, we certainly agree that we have a role in deciding the trajectory of the world, and in so doing, we get to think which critique to advance.

We have argued the law is not a neutral body. It corresponds to an anthropological principle, and the results of that law are also corresponsive to that anthropological principle. The anthropological principle behind *A.J.T v. Osseo Area Schools* is that people with disabilities, particularly children with disabilities, have the same right to education as children without disabilities. The differences between the children do not change their rights-based claims. Even as the Courts appear to recognize the dignity of children with disabilities, the dignity of difference regarding gender identity is not receiving similar treatment.

As of May 6, 2025, the Supreme Court allowed the Trump administration's ban on transgender people in the military to move forward.[29] The Trump administration advanced the ban after the Executive Order "Defending Women from Gender Ideology Extremism and Restoring Biological Truth to the Federal Government," which states that the federal government will only recognize gender on the basis of sex.[30] Importantly, a bi-morphic conception of sex that has no room for intersex people. The anthropological principles of the law in terms of gender identity are becoming increasingly rigid, erasing transgender people from civic and public aspects of society such as the military and education. These erasures express a conception of humanity that is categorically binary. Yet, this is the same Court which included protections of transgender people under Title VII in *Bostock v. Clayton County*. Transgender people occupy a mixed status in American law, at once protected against sex discrimination, yet also unable to participate in some aspects of life. This confusion places transgender people in a precarious situation, highly visible as the new Lavender Scare pursues an agenda of erasure.

The law, then, cannot always be trusted as a tool for progress. What do we do outside of the law? Ultimately this is the question that confronts us as we think of a future which celebrates difference. It is imperative to maintain a balance of both theory and praxis. Actions in the courts ought to adopt a social model of care to pursue avenues that reify an anthropological principle of difference and vulnerability. The theory which drives the law must embrace and celebrate vulnerability, examining the ways in which our futures are enmeshed. As disability justice activists have long said—nothing about us without us.

Notes

1. Alan Hyde, 11.
2. Pheng Cheah and Elizabeth Grosz, "The Body of the Law: Notes Toward a Theory of Corporate Justice," *Thinking Through the Body of the Law* (1996): 19–20.
3. Khiara M. Bridges, *The Poverty of Privacy Rights*; Roberts, Dorothy. *Killing the Black Body: Race, Reproduction, and the Meaning of Liberty*. New York: Vintage Books, 1998.
4. Simone Weil, 50, 53.
5. Eli Clare, *Exile and Pride: Disability, Queerness, and Liberation* (Durham, NC: Duke University Press, 2015).
6. Carol Gilligan, *In a Different Voice.*
7. John W. Borkowski, Aleks Ostojic Rushing, and Samantha Bowie, "Supreme Court to Hear Case on Legal Standard for Cases Brought by Students with Disabilities," *Husch Blackwell*, February 20, 2025, https://www.k-12legalinsights.com/2025/02/supreme-court-to-hear-case-on-legal-standard-for-cases-brought-by-students-with-disabilities/.

8. Katherine Schaeffer, "What Federal Education Data Show About Students with Disabilities in the U.S.," *PEW Research Center*, July 24, 2023, https://www.pewresearch.org/short-reads/2023/07/24/what-federal-education-data-shows-about-students-with-disabilities-in-the-us/.
9. This has often been done in tandem with attacks on diversity, equity, and inclusion efforts (with "accessibility" sometimes added to DEI) and with coordinated efforts alongside red states to target transgender protections under the Rehabilitation Act Section 504.
10. "Fact Sheets: President Donald J. Trump Ends DEI Madness and Restores Excellence and Safety within the Federal Aviation Administration," *The White House*, January 22, 2025, https://www.whitehouse.gov/fact-sheets/2025/01/fact-sheet-president-donald-j-trump-ends-dei-madness-and-restores-excellence-and-safety-within-the-federal-aviation-administration/.
11. "Leading Disability Organizations: Blame of Deadly Crash on Disabled Federal Workers is Baseless, Irresponsible," *National Disability Rights Network*, January 30, 2025, https://www.ndrn.org/resource/dca-crash/.
12. "Defending Women from Gender Ideology Extremism and Restoring Biological Truth to the Federal Government," *The White House*, January 20, 2025, https://www.whitehouse.gov/presidential-actions/2025/01/defending-women-from-gender-ideology-extremism-and-restoring-biological-truth-to-the-federal-government/.
13. Carla K. Johnson, "Health Info Wiped from Federal Websites Following Trump Order Targeting Transgender Rights," *PBS*, January 31, 2025, https://www.pbs.org/newshour/health/health-info-wiped-from-federal-websites-following-trump-order-targeting-transgender-rights
14. Ibid.; Lisa Francois, "The Human Toll of Trump's Anti-Trans Crusade," *ACLU*, April 3, 2025, https://www.aclu.org/news/lgbtq-rights/the-human-toll-of-trumps-anti-trans-crusade; Geoff Mulvihill, "6 Ways Trump's Executive Orders are Targeting Transgender People," *PBS*, February 1, 2025, https://www.pbs.org/newshour/politics/6-ways-trumps-executive-orders-are-targeting-transgender-people.

15. "Defending Women from Gender Ideology Extremism."
16. Ibid.
17. Ibid.
18. *Perkins et al. v. State* (HB 121), *ACLU,* https://www.aclu.org/cases/perkins-et-al-v-state.
19. "Legal Challenges to President Trump's Anti-LGBTQ+ Executive Orders," *GLAD Law,* https://www.glad.org/legal-challenges-to-trumps-anti-lgbtq-executive-orders/.
20. Lyndon B. Johnson, "The State of the Union Address," *The American Presidency Project,* https://www.presidency.ucsb.edu/node/242292.
21. Adam Smith, *The Theory of Moral Sentiment,* The Project Gutenberg eBook, https://www.gutenberg.org/cache/epub/67363/pg67363-images.html.
22. Mel Y. Chen, *Chronic Illness, Slowness, and the Time of Writing* (New York: NYU Press, 2023).
23. Martha Nussbaum, "Capabilities as Fundamental Entitlements: Sen and Social Justice," *Feminist Economics* 9(2003): 41–42.
24. Jonathan Herring, *Caring and the Law,* 175.
25. Tina Vaittinen, "An Ethics of Needs: Deconstructing Neoliberal Biopolitics and Care Ethics with Derrida and Spivak," *Philosophies (Basel)* 7, no.4(2022): 73; Tina Vaittinen, "The Power of the Vulnerable Body: A New Political Understanding of Care," *International Feminist Journal of Politics* 17,no.1(2014): 100–118; Giorgia Agamden, *Homo Sacer: Sovereign Power and Bare Life* (Standford University Press: Standford CA, 1998).
26. Lee Edelman, *No Future: Queer Theory and the Death Drive* (Duke University Press, 2004).
27. Which would necessitate an interrogation of the State as a colonial force rooted in racial and carceral capitalism, a system that depends on the disposability of certain populations for capital.
28. Bernard E. Harcourt, *Critique & Praxis: A Critical Philosophy of Illusions, Values, and Action* (New York: Columbia University Press, 2020), 252.
29. April Rubin, "Trump Administration Can Enforce Transgender Military Ban, Supreme Court Says," *Axios,* May 6, 2025, https://www.axios.com/2025/05/06/transgender-military-ban-scotus-trump.
30. "Defending Women from Gender Ideology Extremism."

References

"Abortion in the United States." *Guttmacher Institute.* June 2024. https://www.guttmacher.org/fact-sheet/induced-abortion-united-states

"A Conversation About Skrmetti With Ezra Young & Naomi Schoenbaum." Assigned Media, July 8, 2025. https://www.assignedmedia.org/breaking-news/skrmetti-interview-ezra\young-naomi-schoenbaum

Adams, Rachel. "Choosing Disability, Visualizing Care." *Kennedy Institute of Ethics Journal* 27,no.2(2017): 301–321.

Adams, Tabitha. "The Progression of the LGBTQ+ Rights Movement in the United States: The Human Rights Campaign." (2019).

Adkins, Judith. "These People Are Frightened to Death: Congressional Investigations and the Lavender Scare." *Prologue* 48, no. 2 (Summer 2016): 6–20.

Agamben, Giorgio. *Homo Sacer: Sovereign Power and Bare Life.* Standford University Press: Standford CA, 1998.

ALM GL ch. 272, § 21.

"American with Disabilities Act," 42(2008).

Amundson, Ron. "Disability, Ideology, and Quality of Life: A Bias in Biomedical Ethics." In *Genetic Testing, Healthcare, and Disability.* Eds. David Wasserman, Jerome Bickerbach, and Robert Wachbrot. Cambridge University Press, 2005.

"Anthony Comstock's 'Chastity' Laws." *PBS.* https://www.pbs.org/wgbh/americanexperience/features/pill-anthony-comstocks-chastity-laws/#:~:text=These%20laws%20stretched%20back%20almost,lewd%2C%20immoral%20and%20promoted%20promiscuity.&text=The%20driving%20force%20behind%20the,New%20Yorker%20named%20Anthony%20Comstock

R. C. Valentine and Z. McNeill, *The Coercive Power of the Law*,
https://doi.org/10.1007/978-3-032-07589-5

"Anti-LGBT Victiminization in the United States." *The Williams Institute*. https://williamsinstitute.law.ucla.edu/publications/anti-lgbt-victimizatio n-us/

a Revolution, Launched. "Facts and Ideas From Anywhere." *Proc (Bayl Univ Med Cent)* 28, no. 3 (2015): 421–432.

Asadi-Pooya, Ali A., Mehdi Bazrafshan, and Mohen Farazdaghi, "Cluster Analysis of a Large Dataset of Patients with Lennox-Gastaut Syndrome," *Seizure* 92(2021): 36–39.

Asch, Adrienne. "Prenatal Diagnosis and Selective Abortion: A Challenge to Practice and Policy." *American Journal of Public Health* 89, no. 11 (1999): 1649–1657.

Auvin, Stéphane et al., "The Impact of Seizure Frequency on Quality of Life in Patients with Lennox-Gastaut Syndrome or Dravet Syndrome." *Epilepsy &* Behavior 123(2021): 108239.

Ballatori, Gaia. "Knowledge Control as a Form of Social Control. From Hermeneutical Injustice to Epistemology of Resistance." *Astrolabio: revista internacional de filosofia* (2022): 47–62.

Baskin, Sienna, Aziza Ahmed, and Anna Forbes. "Criminal laws on sex work and HIV transmission: Mapping the laws, considering the consequences." *Denv. L. Rev.* 93 (2015): 355.

Baynton, Douglas C. "Disability and the Justification of Inequality in American History." *The Disability Studies Reader* 17, no.33(2013): 33–57.

Beauchamp, Toby. *Going Stealth: Transgender Politics and U.S. Surveillance Practices*. Durham, NC: Duke University Press, 2019.

Bethel Sch. Dist. v. Fraser. 478 U.S. 675, 677.

Bd. of Trs. v. Garrett. 531 U.S. 356, 367.

Borkowski, John W., Aleks Ostojic Rushing, and Samantha Bowie. "Supreme Court to Hear Case on Legal Standard for Cases Brought by Students with Disabilities," *Husch Blackwell*, February 20, 2025, https://www.k-12legalin sights.com/2025/02/supremecourt-to-hear-case-on-legal-standard-for-cases-brought-by-students-with-disabilities/

Brewer, Michael E. "Sodomy Laws and Privacy-The Cost of Keeping Gays in the Closet." *Denv. UL Rev.* 79 (2001): 546.

Bridges, Khiara. *The Poverty of Privacy Rights*. Stanford University Press, 2017.

Brier, Jennifer. *Infectious Ideas: U.S. Political Responses to the AIDS Crisis*. Chapel Hill: University of North Carolina Press, 2009.

Broun, Heywood, and Margaret Leech. *Anthony Comstock, Roundsman of the Lord*. A. & C. Boni, 1927.

Brown, Camille, Carolyn M. Porta, Marla E. Eisenberg, Barbara J. McMorris, and Renee E. Sieving. "Family relationships and the Health and Well-being of Transgender and Gender-Diverse Youth: A Critical Review." *LGBT health* 7, no. 8 (2020): 407–419.

Bryant, Anita. *The Anita Bryant Story: The Survival of Our Nation's Families and the Threat of Militant Homosexuality.* Old Tappan, New Jersey: Revell, 1977.

Bryant, Anita, and Bob Green. *At Any Cost.* Old Tappan, New Jersey: Revell, 1978.

Burdick, Kendall J. et al. "Abortion Restrictiveness and Infant Mortality: An Ecologic Study, 2014–2018." https://www.ajpmonline.org/article/S0749-3797(23)00408-7/fulltext

Burnette, Brandon R. "Comstock Act of 1873." *The Free Speech Center.* https://firstamendment.mtsu.edu/article/comstock-act-of-1873/ (last visited Jun 5, 2024).

Burris, Scott. "Legal aspects of regulating bathhouses: cases from 1984 to 1995." In *Gay Bathhouses and Public Health Policy*, pp. 131–151. Routledge, 2013.

Burris, Scott. "Testing, Disclosure, and the Right to Privacy." In *AIDS Law Today: A New Guide for the Public*, edited by Scott Burris, Harlon L. Dalton, Judith Leonie Miller, and Yale AIDS Law Project, 115–49. Yale University Press, 1993.

Butler, Judith. *Bodies That Matter: On the Discursive Limits of Sex.* New York: Routledge, 1993.

Butler, Judith. *Undoing Gender.* New York: Routledge, 2004.

Campbell, Maya. "Perceived to Be Deviant": Social Norms, Social Change, and New York State's" Walking While Trans "Ban." *Cal. L. Rev.* 110 (2022): 1065.

Canaday, Margot. *The Straight State: Sexuality and Citizenship in Twentieth Century America.* Princeton, NJ: Princeton University Press, 2009.

Chae, Sophia, Sheila Desai, Marjorie Crowell, and Gilda Sedgh. "Reasons Why Women have Induced Abortions: A Synthesis of Findings from 14 Countries." *Contraception* 96, no. 4 (2017): 233–241.

Cheah, Pheng, David Fraser, and Judith Grbich, eds. *Thinking Through the Body of the Law.* New York University Press, 1996.

Chen, Mel Y. *Chronic Ills, Slowness, and the Time of Writing.* New York: NYU Press, 2023.

Cingel, Drew P., Sindy R. Sumter, and Jiska van de Leur. "The Role of Social Context During Television on Children's Moral Judgements about Social Exclusion and Stigmatization of Others." *Media Psychology* 22, no.1(2019): 133–51.

City of Chicago v. Wilson, 389 N.E. 2d 522 (Ill. 1978).

City of Cincinnati v. Adams, 330 N.E. 2d 463 (Ohio Municipal Court 1974).

City of Grants Pass v. Johnson, 219 L. Ed. 2d 941, 974.

City of New York v. New St. Mark's Baths, 130 Misc. 2d 911, 497 N.Y.S. 2d 979 (N.Y. Sup. Ct. Jan. 6, 1986).

Clare, Eli. *Exil and Pride: Disability, Queerness, and Liberation*. Durham, NC: Duke University Press, 2015.

Clare, Eli. "Stolen Bodies, Reclaimed Bodies: Disability and Queerness." *Public Culture* 13, no. 3 (2001): 359–365.

Closson, Kalysha, Sabrina C. Boyce, Nicole Johns, David J. Inwards-Breland, Edwin Elizabeth Thomas, and Anita Raj. "Physical, Sexual, and Intimate Partner Violence Among Transgender and Gender-Diverse Individuals." *JAMA network open* 7, no. 6 (2024): e2419137.

Coco, Adrienne Phelps. "Diseased, Maimed, Mutilated: Categorizations of Disability and an Ugly Law in Late Nineteenth-Century Chicago." *Journal of Social History* 44, no.1(2010): 23–37.

Cohen, Adam. *Imbeciles: The Supreme Court, American Eugenics, and the Sterilization of Carrie Buck*. Penguin Books, 2017.

Columbus v. Rogers, 324 N.E.2d 563 (Ohio 1975).

Cooper, Melinda. *Family Values: Between Neoliberalism and the New Social Conservatism*. New York: Zone Books, 2017.

Copelon, Rhonda and Sylvia Ann Law. "'Nearly Allied to Her Right to Be'-Medicaid Funding for Abortion: The Story of *Harris v. McRae*." *WOMENS & THE LAW STORIES* (2010): 207.

Cui, W., R. Kobau, M. M. Zack, J. M. Buelow, and K. A. Joan. "Recent Changes in Attitudes of US Adults toward People with Epilepsy—Results from the 2005 Summer Styles and 2013 Fall Styles Surveys." *Epilepsy & Behavior* 52(2015): 108–118.

Davis, Khyree D. "Transnational blackness at Toronto Pride: queer disruption as theory and method." *Gender, Place & Culture* 28, no. 11 (2021): 1541–1560.

Dawson, Lindsey, Jennifer Kates, Alex Montero, and Ashley Kirzinger. "LGBTQ+ Health Policy." *KFF*. September 30, 2024, https://www.kff.org/health-policy-101-lgbtq-healthpolicy/?entry=table-of-contents-introduction

Dayapoglu, Nuray, Neşe İşcan Ayyıldız, Demet Şeker, "Fear of Negative Evaluation and the Concealment of Their Disease by Epilepsy Patients," *Epilepsy & Behavior* 113(2020).

Death Penalty Information Center, "Criminalization of Homosexuality in American History," last modified September 25, 2024, https://deathpenaltyinfo.org/policy-issues/biases-andvulnerabilities/lgbtq-people/criminalization-of-homosexuality-in-american-history.

Declercq, Eugene et al. "The U.S. Maternal Health Divide: The limited maternal health services and worse outcomes of states proposing new abortion restrictions Abortion Restrictions Affect Mortality Rate." *Commonwealth Fund*. https://www.commonwealthfund.org/publications/issue-briefs/2022/dec/us-maternalhealth-divide-limited-services-worse-outcomes

"Defending Women from Gender Ideology Extremism and Restoring Biological Truth to the Federal Government." *The White House*. January 20, 2025. https://www.whitehouse.gov/presidential-actions/2025/01/defending-women-fromgender-ideology-extremism-and-restoring-biological-truth-to-the-federal-government/

D'emilio, John, and Estelle B. Freedman. *Intimate Matters: A History of Sexuality in America*. University of Chicago Press, 1997.

De Orio, Scott. "Bad queers: LGBTQ people and the Carceral State in modern America." *Law & Social Inquiry* 47, no. 2 (2022): 691–711.

de Sousa, Tanya et al. "The 2023 Annual Homelessness Assessment Report (AHAR) to Congress." *The U.S. Department of Housing and Urban Development*. December 2023. https://www.huduser.gov/portal/sites/default/files/pdf/2023-ahar-part-1.Pdf.

de Souza, Jéssica Lopes, Aline Scardoeli Faiola, Carmen Silvia Molleis Galego Miziara, and Maria Luiza Giraldes de Manreza. "The Perceived Social Stigma of People with Epilepsy with Regard to the Question of Employability." *Neurology Research International* 2018, no. 1 (2018): 4140508.

Diamant, Jeff, Besheer Mohamed and Rebecca Leppert. "What the Data Says About Abortion in the U.S." *PEW Research Center.* March 25 2024. https://www.pewresearch.org/shortreads/2024/03/25/what-the-data-says-about-abortion-in-the-us/

"Disability Characteristics." *Census*. https://data.census.gov/table?q=disability

Dobbs v. Jackson Women's Health Org., 2247.

Double Scorpio. https://doublescorpio.com/?fbclid=PAZXh0bgNhZW0CMTEAAaY4BzoyRajbb8Qn4g5lcsmlE2eUfXWGWfknOpUFd_u9pJHBzdROZoePoFk_aem_xgBcYt2N36DfysMTYluTJg.

Drag Story Hour. https://www.dragstoryhour.org/

Dunn, Ethan, "Silencing and Surveillance: The Struggle of Same-Sex Desire in the Shadow of the 20thCentury Police State" (2024). Honors Theses. 669.

Edelman, Lee. *No Future: Queer Theory and the Death Drive*. Durham, NC: Duke University Press, 2004.

Eisenstadt v. Baird, 405 U.S. 438

Englehardt, H. Tristam Jr. *The Foundations of Bioethics*. 2nd Edition. New York: Oxford University Press, 1996.

Eskridge Jr, William N. "Challenging the Apartheid of the Closet: Establishing Conditions for Lesbian and Gay Intimacy, Nomos, and Citizenship, 1961–1981." *Hofstra L. Rev.* 25 (1996): 817.

Eskridge Jr., William N. *Dishonorable Passions: Sodomy laws in America, 1861–2003.* New York: Viking, 2008.

Eskridge Jr, William N. "Law and the construction of the closet: American regulation of same sex intimacy, 1880–1946." *Iowa L. Rev.* 82 (1996): 1007.

Evans-Marshall v. Bd. of Educ. of Tipp City Exempted Vill. Sch. Dist. 624 F.3d 332 (6th Cir. 2010).

Biden. "Fact Sheets: President Donald J. Trump Ends DEI Madness and Restores Excellence and Safety within the Federal Aviation Administration." *The White House*. January 22, 2025. https://www.whitehouse.gov/fact-sheets/2025/01/fact-sheet-president-donald-j-trumpends-dei-madness-and-restores-excellence-and-safety-within-the-federal-aviationadministration/

"FBI Releases 2022 Crime in the Nation Statistics." *FBI*. October 16, 2023. https://www.fbi.gov/news/press-releases/fbi-releases-2022-crime-in-the-nation-statistics.

Fingerhut, Hannah. "Iowa's Civil-Rights Protections No Longer Include Gender Identity as New Law Takes Effect." *Associated Press*, July 1, 2025. https://apnews.com/article/iowa-civilrights-code-gender-identity-d90d374e821b5663b8114eef27e8d03d

Fischer, Mia. *Terrorizing Gender: Transgender Visibility and the Surveillance Practices of the U.S. Security State*. Lincoln: University of Nebraska Press, 2019.

Fla. Stat. § 1000.071.

Foist, Hunter. "Keep Saying Gay: How Nationwide" Don't Say Gay "Bills Violate the First Amendment, Chill Protected Speech, and Hinder Public Health Outcomes." *Ind. Health L. Rev.* 21 (2024): 177.

Foster, Diana Greene. *The Turnaway Study: Ten Years, a Thousand Women, and the Consequences of Having – or Being Denied – an Abortion*. Simon and Schuster, 2021.

Foster, Diana Greene, et al., "Effects of Carrying an Unwanted Pregnancy to Term on Women's Existing Children." *The Journal of Pediatrics* vol. 205 (2019): 183–189. https://doi.org/10.1016/j.jpeds.2018.09.026

Foucault, Michel. *Discipline and Punish: The Birth of the Prison*. Translated by Alan Sheridan. New York: Vintage Books, 1995

Foucault, Michel. *The History of Sexuality Volume I*. New York: Pantheon Books, 1978.

Francois, Lisa. "The Human Toll of Trump's Anti-Trans Crusade." *ACLU*. April 3, 2025. https://www.aclu.org/news/lgbtq-rights/the-human-toll-of-trumps-anti-trans-crusade

Gabrielle, Vincent. "UConn Study: Why Being Outed as LGBTQ Is Bad for Youth Mental Health." *CT Insider*. April 21, 2024. https://www.ctinsider.com/news/article/ct-lgbtqouted-youth-mental-health-uconn-study-19398381.php.

Garland-Thomson, Rosemarie. "Misfits: A Feminist Materialist Disability Concept." *Hypatia* 26. No.3(2011): 591–609.

Garland-Thomson, Rosemarie. "Theorizing Disability." *Extraordinary Bodies: Figuring Physical Disability in American Culture and Literature* (1997): 19–54.

Gilligan, Carol. *In a Different Voice: Moral Psychology and Women's Development.* Cambridge: Harvard University Press, 1982.

GLSEN. "Laws that Prohibit the 'Promotion of Homosexuality': Impacts and Implications." https://www.glsen.org/sites/default/files/2019-12/No_Promo_Homo_2018.pdf.

Goffman, Erving. "Stigma and Social Identity." In *Deviance & Liberty.* Routledge, 2018. 24–31.

Kennedy. Supreme Court of the United States, "Gonzalez v. Carhart," 2007, https://supreme.justia.com/cases/federal/us/550/124/

Goodman, Ryan. "Beyond the enforcement principle: Sodomy laws, social norms, and social panoptics." *Calif. L. Rev.* 89 (2001): 643.

Goodwin, Cal. "The Unsung Heroines of Stonewall." *National Parks Conservation Association* (blog). March 27, 2025. https://www.npca.org/articles/2736-the-unsung-heroines-ofstonewall

Gordon, Linda, and Bonnie Mass. "Woman's Body, Woman's Right: A Social History of Birth Control in America." *Science and Society* 42, no. 3 (1978).

Greey, Ali. "Queer inclusion precludes (Black) queer disruption: Media analysis of the Black lives matter Toronto sit-in during Toronto Pride 2016." In *Leisure, Racism, and National Populist Politics*, pp. 15–29. Routledge, 2021.

Griswold v. Connecticut, 381 U.S. 479.

Gross, Aeyal. "Gender Outlaws Before the Law: The Courts of the Borderlands." *Dukeminier Awards: Best Sexual Orientation & Gender Identity L. Rev.* 9(2010): 159.

Gunja, Munira Z., Evan D. Gumas & Reginald D. Williams, "The U.S. maternal mortality crisis continues to worsen: An international comparison Maternal Mortality Rate in U.S. Worsens." *Commonwealth Fund.* https://www.commonwealthfund.org/blog/2022/usmaternal-mortality-crisis-continues-worsen-internationalcomparison#:~:text=New%20international%20data%20show%20the,most%20other%20high%2Dincome%20countries

Habteselasse, Sham and Sam LaFrance. "What Students Lose When School Becomes a Political Battleground." *American Civil Liberties Union.* February 20, 2025. https://www.aclu.org/news/free-speech/what-students-lose-when-school-becomes-apolitical-battleground

Halley, Janet E. "Reasoning about sodomy: Act and identity in and after Bowers v. Hardwick."| *Va. L. Rev.* 79 (1993): 1721.

Hamilton, Blair, Andrew Brown, Stephanie Montagner-Moraes, Cristina Comeras-Chueca, Peter G. Bush, Fergus M. Guppy, and Yannis P. Pitsiladis. "Strength, Power and Aerobic Capacity of Transgender Athletes: A

Cross-sectional Study." *British Journal of Sports Medicine* 58, no. 11 (2024): 586–597.

Harcourt, Bernard E. *Critique & Praxis: A Critical Philosophy of Illusions, Values, and Action.* New York: Columbia University Press, 2020.

Haritaworn, Jin, Adi Kuntsman, and Silvia Posocco. "Introduction." in *Queer Necropolitics.* Ed. Jin Haritaworn, Adi Kuntsman, and Silvia Posocco. Abingdon, Oxon: Routledge, 2014. https://doi.org/10.4324/9780203798300.

Harris, Kyle. "Denver Contracts with Homeless Shelters that Discriminate Against Disabled People, Advocates Say." *Denverite.* December 27, 2024. https://denverite.com/2024/12/27/denver-shelters-disability-discrimination-lawsuit/

Harris v. McRae, 448 U.S. 297 (1980).

Herring, Jonathan. *Caring and the Law.* Portland, Oregon: Hart Publishing, 2013.

Herring, Jonathan. "Ethics of care and the public good of abortion." *U. Oxford Hum. Rts. Hub J.* (2019): 1.

Hirschmann, Nancy J. "Disability as a New Frontier for Feminist Intersectionality Research." *Politics & Gender* 8, no.3(2012): 396–405.

Hodge Jr, James G., Jennifer L. Piatt, Erica N. White, Summer Ghaith, and Madisyn Puchebner. "Curbing Reversals of Non-Textual Constitutional Rights." *U. Md. LJ Race, Religion, Gender & Class* 22 (2022): 167.

Hoppe, Trevor. *Punishing Disease: HIV and the Criminalization of Sickness.* Berkeley: University of California Press, 2018.

Horowitz, Helen Lefkowitz. "Rereading sex: Battles over sexual knowledge and suppression in nineteenth-century America." (2002).

"How Many Adults and Youth Identify as Transgender in the United States?" *Williams Institute.* https://williamsinstitute.law.ucla.edu/publications/trans-adults-united-states/

"Interactive map: US abortion policies and access after Roe." *Guttmacher Institute.* https://states.guttmacher.org/policies/

Jóhannsdóttir, Ásta, S.T. Egilson, and K. Runswick-Cole, "Feeling Disability: Theories of Affect and Critical Disability Studies." *Disability & Society* 33, no2(2018): 197–217.

Johnson, Carla K. "Health Info Wiped from Federal Websites Following Trump Order Targeting Transgender Rights." *PBS.* January 31, 2025. https://www.pbs.org/newshour/health/health-info-wiped-from-federal-websitesfollowing-trump-order-targeting-transgender-rights

Johnson, Lyndon B. "The State of the Union Address." *The American Presidency Project.* https://www.presidency.ucsb.edu/node/242292

Jones, Philip Edward. "Respectability politics and straight support for LGB rights." *Political Research Quarterly* 75, no. 4 (2022): 935–949.

Kane, Desiree and Jen Byers. "Amid Legacies of Colonial and Anti-Trans Harm, Two-Spirits Struggle for Safety: This Trans Day of Remembrance, We Are Holding Nex Benedict and All Two-Spirit People in Our Hearts." *Truthout*. November 20, 2023. https://truthout.org/articles/amid-legacies-of-colonial-and-anti-trans-harm-two-spiritsstruggle-for-safety/.

Katz, Jonathan. "Love stories: Sex between men before homosexuality." *(No Title)* (2001).

Kim, Seung Min. "Biden blames Trump for Florida's 6-week abortion ban, says women nationwide face Health Crisis." *AP News*. https://apnews.com/article/president-joe-bidenflorida-donald-trump-abortion-6b069fd8c14c4c65236d708b347697f0

Kim, Juliana. "Park Service Erases 'Transgender' on Stonewall Website, Uses the Term 'GB' Movement." *National Public Radio*. February 14, 2025,https://www.npr.org/2025/02/14/g-s1-48923/stonewall-monument-transgender-parkservice

Kimport, Katrina. *No Real Choice: How Culture and Politics Matter for Reproductive Autonomy*. New Jersey: Rutgers University Press, 2022.

King, Charles R. "Abortion in nineteenth century America: A conflict between women and their physicians." *Women's health issues: official publication of the Jacobs Institute of Women's Health* 2, no. 1 (1992): 32–39.

Kissiov, Djem, Taylor Dewall, and Bruce Hermann, "The Ohio Hospital for Epileptics – The First 'Epilepsy Colony' in America," *Epilepsia* 54, no.4(2013): 1524–1534.

Kittay, Eva Feder. "Anita Silvers, David Wasserman, and Mary B. Mahowald. Disability, Difference, and Discrimination: Perspectives on Justice in Bioethics and Public Policy. New York, Rowman & Littlefield, 1998," *Hypatia* 17, no. 1 (2002): 209–213.

Kittay, Eva Feder. *Learning from My Daughter: The Value and Care of Disabled Minds*. Oxford University Press: 2019.

Kittay, Eva Feder. "The Personal is Philosophical is Political: A Philosopher and Mother of a Cognitively Disabled Person Sends Notes from the Battlefield." *Metaphilosophy* 40, no. 3–4 (2009): 606–627.

Lakshmeeramya, Malladi. "The People of the State of *New York v. Margaret H. Sanger*." *Embryo Project Encyclopedia*. https://embryo.asu.edu/pages/people-state-new-york-vmargaret-h-sanger-1918 (last visited Jun 5, 2024).

Lakshmeeramya, Malladi. "United States v. One Package of Japanese Pessaries." *Embryo Project Encyclopedia*. https://embryo.asu.edu/pages/united-states-v-one-packagejapanese-pessaries-1936.

Lavietes, Matt. "Florida School Districts Removed Roughly 300 Books Last School Year." *NBC News*. September 12, 2023. https://www.nbcnews.com/nbc-out/out-news/florida-schooldistricts-removed-roughly-300-books-last-school-year-rcna104367.

Lawrence v. Texas, 539 U.S. 558 (2003)
"Leading Disability Organizations: Blame of Deadly Crash on Disabled Federal Workers is Baseless, Irresponsible." *National Disability Rights Network.* January 30, 2025. https://www.ndrn.org/resource/dca-crash/
"Legal Challenges to President Trump's Anti-LGBTQ+ Executive Orders." *GLAD Law.* https://www.glad.org/legal-challenges-to-trumps-anti-lgbtq-executive-orders/
Lehtinen, Ullaliina. "How Does One Know What Shame is? Epistemology, Emotions, and Forms of Life in Juxtaposition." *Hypatia* 13, no.1(1998): 56–77.
"LGBT+ Pride 2023." *Ipsos.* https://www.ipsos.com/sites/default/files/ct/news/documents/202305/Ipsos%20LGBT%2B%20Pride%202023%20Global%20Survey%20Report%20%20rev.pdf
Lindemann, Hilde. "'… But I Could Never Have One": The Abortion Intuition and Moral Luck." *Hypatia* 24, no. 1 (2009): 41–55.
Lombardo, Paul A. *Three Generations, No Imbeciles: Eugenics, The Supreme Court, and* Buck v. Bell. Baltimore: Johns Hopkins University Press, 2022.
Loving v. Virginia, 388 U.S. 1.
"Lucy Hicks Anderson." *Legacy Project Chicago.* https://legacyprojectchicago.org/person/lucyhicks-anderson
Lugg, Catherine A. "Thinking About Sodomy: Public Schools, Legal Panopticons, and Queers." *Educational Policy*, no. 1 (2006), 39.
Ma, Brandy B. et al. "Regulating Drivers with Epilepsy in Maryland: Results of the Application of a United States Consensus Guideline," *Epilepsia* 58, no.8(2017): 1389–1397.
Magni, Gabriele. "Nearly 240 Anti-LGBTQ Bills Filed in 2022 So Far, With Most Targeting Trans People." *NBC News*, March 20, 2022. https://www.nbcnews.com/nbc-out/outpolitics-and-policy/nearly-240-anti-lgbtq-bills-filed-2022-far-targeting-trans-peoplercna20418
Malatino, Hil. *Trans Care.* Minneapolis: University of Minnesota Press, 2020.
Malik, Najma Iqbal et al., "Perceived Stigma, Discrimination and Psychological Problems Among Patients with Epilepsy," *Front Psychiatry* (2022).
Mangold, Evelyn. "The Viral Injustice of HIV Criminalization." *The Regulatory Review.* February 24, 2022, https://www.theregreview.org/2022/02/24/mangold-viral-injusticehiv-criminalization/
Markovish, Matt. "Police Deny LGBTQ Bar Visits Were Raids; Officials Change Lewd Laws," *MyNorthwest*, January 31, 2024. https://mynorthwest.com/local/police-deny-lgbtq-barvisits-raids-officials-change-lewd-laws/3948822.
Mbembe, Achille. "Necropolitics." *Public Culture* 15, no. 1 (2003): 11–40.
McArthur, James B. "As the tide turns: the changing HIV/AIDS epidemic and the criminalization of HIV exposure." *Cornell L. Rev.* 94 (2008): 707.

McNeill, Zane. "Denver Schools Face Federal Inquiry Over All-Gender Restroom." *Truthout*, January 29, 2025. https://truthout.org/articles/denver-schools-face-federal-inquiry-overall-gender-restroom/

McNeill, Zane. "From Courts to Community Power: Trans Rights Advocates Respond to Skrmetti's Fallout." Nonprofit Quarterly, August 4, 2025. https://nonprofitquarterly.org/from-courts-to-community-power-trans-rights-advocatesrespond-to-skrmettis-fallout/

McNeill, Zane. "How the Trump Administration Is Undermining Civil Rights Law—and How Nonprofits Can Fight Back." *Nonprofit Quarterly*, April 14, 2025. https://nonprofitquarterly.org/how-the-trump-administration-is-undermining-civil-rightslaw-and-how-nonprofits-can-fight-back/

McNeill, Zane. "Stacking the Courts against Mifepristone." *Political Research Associates*, February 12, 2025. https://politicalresearch.org/2025/02/12/stacking-courts-againstmifepristone

McNeill, Zane. "USDA Suspends Maine Education Funds Over State's Support for Trans Athletes." *Truthout*, April 3, 2025. https://truthout.org/articles/usda-suspends-maineeducation-funds-over-states-support-for-trans-athletes/

McNeill, Zane. "Want to Honor Trans Day of Visibility? Fight With Us Like Your Life Hinges on It." *Truthout*, March 31, 2025. https://truthout.org/articles/want-to-honor-trans-day-ofvisibility-fight-with-us-like-your-life-hinges-on-it/

McNeill, Zane, and Blu Buchanan. "Tracing the Color of Queer Choreopolitics." *The Activist History Review*, January 13, 2020, https://activisthistory.com/2020/01/13/tracing-thecolor-of-queer-choreopolitics

McNeill, Zane, and Kyra Smith. "Whose Pride Is This Anyway? The Quare Performance of the# Black Pride4." In *The Palgrave Handbook of Queer and Trans Feminisms in Contemporary Performance*, pp. 203–222. Cham: Springer International Publishing, 2021.

Medina, Gisselle, "LGBTQ+ Books Bans are Hitting California Schools." *Los Angeles Times*. August 10, 2023. https://www.latimes.com/california/story/2023-08-10/lgbtq-book-bansare-hitting-california-schools-how-teachers-can-fight-back

Meyer v. Nebraska, 262 U.S. 390.

Miller v. California413 U.S. 15, 24 (1973).

Miller, Sarah, Laura R. Wherry, and Diana Greene Foster. "What Happens After an Abortion Denial? A Review of Results from the Turnaway Study." *AEA Papers and Proceedings*, vol. 110 (2014): 226–230.

Monteil, Abby. "Pete Buttigieg Says Trans Athletes in Women's Spots Raise 'Serious Fairness Issues.'" *Them*. July 29, 2025.

Morris, Anne. "Once upon a time in a hospital... the cautionary tale of St George's Health Care NHS Trust v. S, R v. Collins and others ex parte S [1998] 3 All ER 673." *Feminist L. Stud.* 7 (1999): 75.

Morris, Athina, and Nexstar Media Wire. "Gov. DeSantis Signs Controversial 'Don't Say Gay' Bill into Law." *KGET*. March 28, 2022. https://www.kget.com/national-news/govdesantis-signs-controversial-dont-say-gay-bill-into-law/amp/

Movement Advancement Project. "Bans on Transgender Youth Participation in Sports." Accessed March 30, 2025. https://www.lgbtmap.org/equalitymaps/youth/sports_participation_bans.

Movement Advancement Project. "Bans on Transgender People Using Public Bathrooms and Facilities According to Their Gender Identity." Accessed March 30, 2025. https://www.lgbtmap.org/equality-maps/youth/school_bathroom_bans.

Movement Advancement Project. "Forced Outing of Transgender Youth in Schools." Accessed March 30, 2025. https://www.lgbtmap.org/equality-maps/youth/forced_outing.

Movement Advancement Project. "LGBTQ Curricular Laws." Accessed March 30, 2025. https://www.lgbtmap.org/equality-maps/curricular_laws

Movement Advancement Project. "The State of Schools for Trans Youth in 2025." *Medium*. February 25, 2025. https://lgbtmap.medium.com/the-state-of-schools-for-trans-youth-in2025-6110a86b3cb7.

Movement Advancement Project. "Under Fire: New MAP Report Details Eight Tactics to Erase LGBTQ People from Schools and Public Life." March 23, 2023. https://www.mapresearch.org/news/2023-press-release-under-fire-report-2.

Mulvihill, Geoff. "6 Ways Trump's Executive Orders are Targeting Transgender People." *PBS*. February 1, 2025. https://www.pbs.org/newshour/politics/6-ways-trumps-executiveorders-are-targeting-transgender-people

Mulvihill, Geoff. "States Sue Trump, Saying He Is Intimidating Hospitals Over Gender Affirming Care for Youth." *Associated Press*, August 1, 2025. https://apnews.com/article/trump-gender-affirming-care-lawsuit-hospitalsdfc156f4bffcf4b6136658207488d17d

Murphy, Lawrence R. "Defining the crime against nature: Sodomy in the United States appeals courts, 1810-1940." *Journal of Homosexuality* 19, no. 1 (1990): 49–66.

Narvaez, Darcia, Tracy Gleason, Christyan Mitchell, and Jennifer Bentley. "Moral Theme Comprehension in Children." *Journal of Educational Psychology* 91, no.3(1999): 477.

Nussbaum, Martha. "Capabilities as Fundamental Entitlements: Sen and Social Justice." *Feminist Economics* 9(2003): 33–59.

Nussbaum, Martha. *Hiding from Humanity: Disgust, Shame, and the Law.* Princeton: Princeton University Press, 2004.

N.Y. Sess. Laws § 430 (1868).

Ochshorn ex rel. v. Ithaca City Sch. Dist., 645 F.3d 533, 536 (2d Cir. 2011).

Oliver, Mike. "The Social Model of Disability: Thirty Years On." *Disability & Society* 28, no.7(2013).

Osborn, Max. "LGBTQIA+ Individuals' Encounters with Police: Contextual Factors, Help Seeking, and Service Needs." ProQuest Dissertations & Theses, 2022, 36.

Osborn, Paige. "'No Justice, No Pride' Protest Highlights Fault Lines in D.C. LGBTQ Community." WAMU. June 11, 2017, accessed August 10, 2025, https://wamu.org/story/17/06/11/no-justice-no-pride-protest-highlights-fault-lines-d-clgbtq-community/.

Owens, Deirdre Cooper. *Medical Bondage: Race, Gender, and the Origins of American Gynecology.* The University of Georgia Press, 2017.

Pabayo, Roman, Amy Ehntholt, Daniel M. Cook, Megan Reynolds, Peter Muennig, and Sze Y. Liu. "Laws Restricting Access to Abortion Services and Infant Mortality Risk in the United States." *International Journal of Environmental Research and Public Health* 17, no. 11 (2020): 3773.

Pendharkar, Eesha. "Florida Just Expanded the 'Don't Say Gay' Law. Here's What You Need to Know." *Education Week.* April 19, 2023. https://www.edweek.org/policy-politics/floridajust-expanded-the-dont-say-gay-law-heres-what-you-need-to-know/2023/04.

Perkins et al. v. State (HB 121). *ACLU.* https://www.aclu.org/cases/perkins-et-al-v-state

Pettys, Todd E. "Serious Value, Prurient Appeal, and "Obscene" Books in the Hands of Children." *Wm. & Mary Bill Rts. J.* 31 (2022): 1003.

Pierce v. Soc'y of Sisters, 268 U.S. 510

Planned Parenthood v. Casey, 505 U.S. 833.

Pohlhaus, Gaile, and John R. Wright. "Using Wittgenstein Critically: A Political Approach to Philosophy." *Political Theory* 30, no. 6 (2002): 800–827.

Price-Feeney M, Green AE, Dorison SH. "Impact of Bathroom Discrimination on Mental Health Among Transgender and Nonbinary Youth. J Adolesc Health." June 68, no6(2021):1142–1147. https://doi.org/10.1016/j.jadohealth.2020.11.001.

Prince v. Massachusetts, 321 U.S. 158

Probyn, Elspeth. *Blush: Faces of Shame.* Minneapolis: University of Minnesota Press, 2005.

"Project 2025: Mandate for Leadership, The Conservative Promise." Edt. Paul Dans and Steven Groves.

Puar, Jasbir K. *The Right to Maim: Debility, Capacity, Disability.* Durham: Duke University Press, 2017.

Pub. L. 96–123, § 109, 93 Stat. 926.

Queer Rights After *Dobbs v. Jackson Women's Health Organization.* 60 San Diego L. Rev. 45.

Rabban, David M. "The Free Speech League, the ACLU, and changing conceptions of free speech in American history." *Stan. L. Rev.* 45 (1992): 47.

Rabin, Judith A. "The AIDS epidemic and gay bathhouses: a constitutional analysis." *Journal of health politics, policy and law* 10, no. 4 (1986): 729–747.

Rafter, Nicole H. "Claims-Making and Socio-Cultural Context in the First U.S. Eugenics Campaign," *Social Problems* 39, no.1(1992): 17–34.

Raj, Senthorun. "Disturbing disgust: Gesturing to the abject in queer cases." In *Queering criminology*, pp. 83–101. London: Palgrave Macmillan UK, 2016.

Raypol, Crystal. "From Acacia to IUDs: The History of Birth Control in the United States." *Healthline.* https://www.healthline.com/health/birth-control/history-of-birth-control (last visited Jun 5, 2024).

Rector, Kevin. "Queer People Have Shaped America." *Los Angeles Times.* June 6, 2024. https://www.latimes.com/california/story/2024-06-06/queer-lgbtq-america-protect-kids

Redburn, Kate. "Before Equal Protection: The Fall of Cross-dressing Bans and the Transgender Legal Movement, 1963–86." *40 Law and History Review* 679(2022).

Reed, Erin. "After Trans People, Trump Now Erasing Bisexual People from Stonewall National Monument." *Erin in the Morning.* July 10, 2025, https://www.erininthemorning.com/p/after-trans-people-trump-now-erasing

Reilly, Kaitlin. "Authors of LGBTQ Books For Youth Speak Out About Being Banned: 'Feels Like an Attack Against My Personhood, Because That Is What It Is'." Apr. 12, 2022. https://www.yahoo.com/lifestyle/banned-books-ya-queer-authors-173156815.html

Reinders, Hans S. *The Future of the Disabled in a Liberal Society.* Notre Dame: University of Notre Dame Press, 2000.

Richard, Lucile. "Pastoral Power, Sovereign Carelessness, and the Social Divisions of Care Work or: What Foucault Can Teach Us about the 'Crisis of Care'." *Foucault Studies* 36, no. 1 (2024): 322–349.

Riley, John. "Alabama Governor Signs Bill to Remove Anti-Gay Language from Sex Education Curriculum." *Metro Weekly.* April 29, 2021. https://www.metroweekly.com/2021/04/alabama-governor-signs-bill-to-remove-antigay-language-from-sex-education-curriculum/

Rinkunas, Susan. "Trump Quietly Made 3 Chilling Moves Against Reproductive Freedom." *Democracy Docket.* March 12, 2025. https://www.democracydocket.com/opinion/trumpquietly-made-3-chilling-moves-against-reproductive-freedom/

Roberts, Dorothy. *Killing the Black Body: Race, Reproduction, and the Meaning of Liberty.* New York: Vintage Books, 1998.

Roe, Stuart. "'Family Support Would Have Been Like Amazing' LGBTQ Youth Experiences with Parental and Family Suppot." *The Family Journal* 25, no.1(2017): 55–62.

Roe v. Wade, 410 U.S. 113.

Rose, Sarah F. *No Right to Be Idle*. UNC Press, 2017.

Rose, Shari. "Lucy Hicks Anderson: Black Transgender Pioneer of the 1940s." *Blurred Bylines*. February 21, 2022. https://blurredbylines.com/articles/lucy-hicks-anderson-blacktransgender-woman/

Rosky, Clifford. "Anti-gay curriculum laws." *Colum. L. Rev.* 117 (2017): 1461.

Rozin, Paul, Jonathan Haidt, and Clark R. McCauley. "Disgust: The Body and Soul Emotion." In *Handbook of Cognition and Emotion*. Ed. T. Dalgleish and M. Power. John Wiley and Sons, 1999. 429–445.

Rubin, April. "Trump Administration Can Enforce Transgender Military Ban, Supreme Court Says." *Axios*. May 6, 2025. https://www.axios.com/2025/05/06/transgender-military-banscotus-trump

Russell, Thomas D. "BUCK v. BELL, Superintendent of State Colony Epileptics and Feeble Minded, 274 US 200 (1927)" *American Legal History-Russell*.

Ryan, Hugh. "How Dressing in Drag Was Labeled a Crime in the 20th Century." *History.com*. June 25, 2019. https://www.history.com/articles/stonewall-riots-lgbtq-drag-three-articlerule.

Ryan, Hugh. "Who's Afraid of Social Contagion?" *Boston Review*, July 31, 2023. https://www.bostonreview.net/articles/whos-afraid-of-social-contagion/

Ryan, Sara and Ulla Räisänen. "'The Brain is Such a Delicate Thing': An Exploration of Fear and Seizures Among Young People with Epilepsy." *Chronic Illness* 8, no.3(2012): 214–224.

San Francisco AIDS Foundation. "Decades after San Francisco Closed Its Gay Bathhouses, a New Law Paves the Way for Their Return." *San Francisco AIDS Foundation*, February 12, 2020. https://www.sfaf.org/collections/breaking-news/decades-after-sanfrancisco-closed-its-gay-bathhouses-a-new-law-paves-the-way-for-their-return/

Sanger, Carol. "The Rise and Fall of a Reproductive Right: Dobbs v. Jackson Women's Health Organization." *Family Law Quarterly* 56, no. 2–3 (2023): 117.

Sears, Clare. *Arresting Dress: Cross-Dressing, Law, and Fascination in Nineteenth-Century San Francisco*. Durham: Duke University Press, 2015.

Sears, Clare. "This Isn't the First Time Conservatives Have Banned Cross-Dressing in America." *Jacobin*. March 15, 2023. https://jacobin.com/2023/03/cross-dressing-law-united-stateshistory-drag-bans

Seaver-Hall, Philip. "School Pronoun Rules and the Compelled-Speech Objection." *Mercer L. Rev.* 75 (2023): 579.

Schaeffer, Katherine. “What Federal Education Data Show About Students with Disabilities in the U.S.” *PEW Research Center*. July 24, 2023. https://www.pewresearch.org/shortreads/2023/07/24/what-federal-education-data-shows-about-students-with-disabilities-inthe-us/

Schwartz, John. “Heredity as a Factor in Epilepsy.” *The Ohio State Institution Journal* 2, no.3(1920): 53–54.

Schweik, Susan. “Kicked to the curb: Ugly law then and now.” *HARV. CR-CLL REV.* 46 (2011): 1–11.

Schweik, Susan. *The Ugly Laws: Disability in Public*. New York: New York University Press, 2009.

Sears, Alan. “30 Years On: The Toronto Bathhouse Raids and Sexual and Gender Liberation.” *Socialist Project*. February 26, 2011, https://socialistproject.ca/2011/02/b471/.

Sedgwick, Eve Kosofsky. *Epistemology of the Closet*. Berkeley: University of California Press, 1990.

Sedgwick, Eve Kosofsky. *Tendencies*. Durham, NC: Duke University Press, 1993.

Sedgwick, Eve Kosofsky. *Touching Feeling: Affect, Pedagogy, Performativity.* Duke University Press, 2003.

Serano, Julia. *Whipping Girl: A Transsexual Woman on Sexism and the Scape-goating of Femininity.* Hachette UK, 2016.

Sharawat, Indar Kumar, et al., “Efficacy and Safety of Corpus Callosotomy and Ketogenic Diet in Children with Lennox-Gastaut Syndrome: A Systematic Review and Meta-analysis,” *Child’s Nervous* System (2021): 1–10.

Sherman, Carter. “Trump Launches Fresh Attacks on US Abortion Rights.” *The Guardian*. March 4, 2025. https://www.democracydocket.com/opinion/trump-quietly-made-3chilling-moves-against-reproductive-freedom/

Skinner v. Oklahoma, 316 U.S. 535

Skinner-Thompson, Scott. “Trans Animus”. Boston College Law Review 65, no.3(2024): 965–1028.

Skinner-Thompson, Scott. “The Faulty Logic behind the Supreme Court’s Failure to Protect Trans Minors.” *New England Journal of Medicine* 393 (2025): 316.

Skinner-Thompson, Scott. “Transgender Disenfranchisement.” *Washington University Law Review* 102 (2025), U of Colorado Law Legal Studies Research Paper No. 25-1 (January 17, 2025).

Smith, Adam. *The Theory of Moral Sentiment.* The Project Gutenberg eBook. https://www.gutenberg.org/cache/epub/67363/pg67363-images.html.

Smith, Priscilla J. “Contraceptive Comstockery: Reasoning from Immorality to Illness in the Twenty-First Century.” *Conn. L. Rev.* 47 (2014): 971.

Smyth, Lisa. “Feminism and Abortion Politics: Choice, Rights, and Reproductive Freedom.” *Women’s Studies International Forum* 25,no.3(2002): 335–345

Snorton, C. Riley. *Black on Both Sides: A Racial History of Trans Identity.* Minneapolis: University of Minnesota Fences, 2017.

Spade, Dean. "Documenting Gender." *Hastings Law Journal* 59,no3(2008): 731–842.

Spade, Dean. "Rethinking Transphobia and Power—Beyond a Rights Framework." In *Normal Life: Administrative Violence, Critical Trans Politics, and the Limits of Law*, 50–72. Revised and Expanded Edition. Durham, NC: Duke University Press, 2015.

Spindelman, Marc. "Symposium: Sexual Orientation, Gender Identity, & the Constitution: Queer Black Trans Politics and Constitutional Originalsim." *ConLawNOW* 13, no. 2 (2021): 5.

Stone, Geoffrey R. "Sex and the First Amendment: The Long and Winding History of Obscenity Law." *First Amend. L. Rev.* 17 (2018): 134.

"Tennessee Senate Bill No.3." https://www.capitol.tn.gov/Bills/113/Amend/HA0011.pdf

"Testimony for PA House of Representatives Judiciary Committee." Claudia Brenner. April 22, 1992 and August 28.1995. https://www.legis.state.pa.us/WU01/LI/TR/Transcripts/1995_0089_0011_TSTMNY.pdf

The Trevor Project. "Anti-Transgender Laws Cause up to 72% Increase in Suicide Attempts Among Transgender and Nonbinary Youth, Study Shows." September 26, 2024. https://www.thetrevorproject.org/blog/anti-transgender-laws-cause-up-to-72-increase-insuicide-attempts-among-transgender-and-nonbinary-youth-study-shows/.

Thompson, Lauren MacIvor, and Kelly O'Donnell. "Contemporary Comstockery: Legal Restrictions on Medication Abortion." *Journal of General Internal Medicine* 37, no. 10 (2022): 2564–2567.

Thompson, Lauren MacIvor. "Mother's friend: Birth control in Nineteenth-century America National Museum of Civil War Medicine (2017)" https://www.civilwarmed.org/birthcontrol/ (last visited Jun 5, 2024).

Tilley, Cristina Carmody. "The First Amendment and the Second Sex." *Ariz. L. Rev.* 65 (2023): 161.

Toorn, Jojanneke van der, Ruthie Pliskin, and Thekla Morgenroth, "Not Quite Over the Rainbow: The Unrelenting and Insidious Nature of Heteronormative Ideology." *Current Opinion in Psychology* 46(2022): 101340. https://doi.org/10.1016/j.copsyc.2022.101340.

Tronto, Joan C. *Caring Democracy: Markets, Equality, and Justice.* New York: New York University Press, 2013.

Trump, Donald J. "Ending Radical Indoctrination in K-12 Schooling." *The White House.* January 29, 2025. https://www.whitehouse.gov/presidential-actions/2025/01/ending-radicalindoctrination-in-k-12-schooling/.

Turner, Felicity M. *Proving Pregnancy: Gender, Law, and Medical Knowledge in Nineteenth century America.* Chapel Hill: University of North Carolina, 2022.

United States v. Skrmetti, 145 S. Ct. 1816, 1881

U.S. Department of Health and Human Services. "A Timeline of HIV and AIDS." HIV.gov, accessed August 9, 2025, https://www.hiv.gov/hiv-basics/overview/history/hiv-and-aidstimeline#year-1987.

Vaid, Urvashi. *Virtual Equality: The Mainstreaming of Gay and Lesbian Politics.* New York: Anchor Books, 1995.

Vaingankar, Janhavi Ajit, Siow Ann Chong, Edimansyah Abdin, Fiona Devi Siva Kumar, Boon Yiang Chua, Rajeswari Sambasivam, Saleha Shafie, Anitha Jeyagurunathan, Esmond Seow, and Mythily Subramaniam. "Understanding the Relationships Between Mental Disorders, Self-Reported Health Outcomes and Positive Mental Health: Findings from a National Survey." *Health and Quality of Life Outcomes* 18 (2020): 1–10.

Vaittinen, Tina. "An Ethics of Needs: Deconstructing Neoliberal Biopolitics and Care Ethics with Derrida and Spivak." *Philosophies (Basel)* 7, no.4(2022): 73.

Vaittinen, Tina. "The Power of the Vulnerable Body: A New Political Understanding of Care." *International Feminist Journal of Politics* 17,no.1(2014): 100–118.

Valentine, Riley Clare. "Their Is No They're: Wittgenstein On Pluralistic Democracy." *Thesis Eleven* 148, no.1(2018): 39–51.

Valentine, Riley Clare. "Who has a Meaningful Life? A Care Ethics Analysis of Selective Trait Abortion." *Medicine, Health Care and Philosophy* 27, no. 2 (2024): 205–216.

Valentine, Riley Clare. "Willful Brains and Absent Minds: A Phenomenological Investigaiton of Fear, Epilepsy, and Willful Being." *Disability & Society.*

Valentine, Riley Clare, and Zane McNeill, "The Libidinal Law: Sexuality and Desire in U.S. Legal Embodiment," Subjectivity 31, no.3(2024): 286–305.

"WATCH: 'Every Abortion is a Tragedy,' RFK Jr. Says." *PBS.* January 29, 2025. https://www.pbs.org/newshour/politics/watch-every-abortion-is-a-tragedy-rfk-jr-says.

Weil, Simone. "Human Personality." In *Simone Weil: An Anthology.* Editor Siân Miles. London: Virago, 1986: 69–98.

Wikler, Daniel. "Persuasion and coercion for Health." *Paternalism* 37 (1983): 42–43.

Wikler, Daniel. "Who should be blamed for being sick?" *Health education quarterly* 14, no. 1 (1987): 11–25.

Wilkins, Brett. "Trump Administration Scrubs Transgender, Queer People From Stonewall Monument Website." *Common Dreams.* February 14, 2025. https://www.commondreams.org/news/stonewall-transgender

Williams, Simon J. "Bodily Dys-order: Desire, Excess and the Transgression of Corporeal Boundaries," *Body & Society* 4, no.2(1998): 59–82.

Williams Institute. "New Executive Order Removes Workplace Protections for More Than 114,000 Transgender Federal Employees and LGBTQ Employees of Federal Contractors." *Williams Institute*. https://williamsinstitute.law.ucla.edu/press/ndprotections-eo-press-release/

Willis, Brianna. "Dozens Arrested During Houston Police Department Raid at La Zona Bar & Lounge and Los Corrales South, Officials Say," ABC13 Houston, May 10, 2025, https://abc13.com/post/dozens-arrested-during-houston-police-department-raid-la-zonabar-lounge-los-corrales-south-officials-say/16376485/.

Wilson, T. Anansi. "Black, Trans(Gressive) Lives: Furtive Blackness & The Surround of Extralegal Violence." *Geo. J. Gender & L.* 26 (2024): 1223.

Wittgenstein, Ludwig. *Philosophical Investigations.* UK: Basic Blackwell, 2009.

Xaykaothao, Doualy. "Protesters Briefly Halt Pride Parade," MPR News, June 25, 2017. https://www.mprnews.org/story/2017/06/25/protesters-briefly-halt-pride-parade

Yıldırım, Zerrin, Devrimsel Harika Ertem, Ayten Ceyhan Dirican, and Sevim Baybaş. "Stigma Accounts for Depression in Patients with Epilepsy." *Epilepsy & Behavior* 78 (2018): 1–6.

Yurcada, Jo, and Jay Valle. "Republicans Introduce National 'Don't Say Gay' Bill to Restrict LGBTQ Discussions in Schools." *NBC News*. October 19, 2022. https://www.nbcnews.com/nbc-out/out-politics-and-policy/national-dont-say-gay-lawrepublicans-introduce-bill-restrict-lgbtq-re-rcna53064.

Zarembka, Arlene, and Katherine M. Franke. "Women in the AIDS Epidemic: A Portrait of Unmet Needs." *Louis U. Pub. L. Rev.* 9 (1990): 519.

"2024 U.S. National Survey on the Mental Health of LGBTQ+ Young People." *The Trevor Project*. https://www.legis.state.pa.us/WU01/LI/TR/Transcripts/1995_0089_0011_TSTMNY.pdf

Index

R. C. Valentine and Z. McNeill, *The Coercive Power of the Law*,
https://doi.org/10.1007/978-3-032-07589-5

GPSR Compliance
The European Union's (EU) General Product Safety Regulation (GPSR) is a set of rules that requires consumer products to be safe and our obligations to ensure this.

If you have any concerns about our products, you can contact us on

ProductSafety@springernature.com

In case Publisher is established outside the EU, the EU authorized representative is:

Springer Nature Customer Service Center GmbH
Europaplatz 3
69115 Heidelberg, Germany

www.ingramcontent.com/pod-product-compliance
Lightning Source LLC
Chambersburg PA
CBHW071541160226
39774CB00002B/45
9783032075888